1.30

An Evolution of Singlehanders

By the same author

What Were They Like to Fly? (*Ian Allan*)
Trimarans—An Introduction (*Adlard Coles Ltd*)
The Lure of the Sea (*Adlard Coles Ltd*)
East Coast Passage (*Longmans, London and Iskry, Poland*)
Trimaran Development (*Adlard Coles Ltd*)
The Multihull Primer (*Adlard Coles Ltd*)

An Evolution
of
Singlehanders

D H Clarke

Stanford Maritime
London

Stanford Maritime Limited
Member Company of the George Philip Group
12 Long Acre London WC2E 9LP

First published in Great Britain 1976
Copyright © D H Clarke 1975
Set in 10/11 pt Times New Roman and printed by
A Wheaton & Co., Exeter

ISBN 0 540 07145 5

For Mollie

Acknowledgements

It would be quite impossible to acknowledge every source of the information contained in this book. Some of it has been in my head since pre-World War II days; other facts were gleaned during the war. In the mid-fifties such people as R G McCloskey, founder of the Slocum Society, John Pflieger, later Commodore of the Slocum Society Sailing Club, and Jim Logan of Philadelphia sent me a great deal of useful material. Then again, many letters which I have had published in various yachting magazines over a period of forty years or so reaped much harvest—though now I'm afraid I cannot put names to all those people with whom I corresponded; more recently, in the sixties, trimaran enthusiasts wrote to me in the same vein, but I no longer have access to their files, as I left the tri business behind me nine years ago.

But as I wrote this book, so did I make new friends all over the world—and I can at least quote their names. So, to those who must remain anonymous I say thanks a lot, and I hope my letter to you gave you as much pleasure as yours did for me. To the following current helpers I can only again repeat thanks a lot, for this book wouldn't have been nearly so comprehensive without your help.

Sven A Hansson of Sweden; Eric Barnes, Norman Cross and Richard Henderson of the USA; Peter H Comstock, Secretary of the Cruising Club of America; Douglas J Ross of New Zealand; the editor and staff of *Die Yacht* (Germany); Frankie and Jeff Clarkson, British freebooters of the sloop *Pile Cap*; Commander W D Æ King, DSO, DSC, RN(Ret.); Krzysztof Baranowski of

Acknowledgements

Poland; Sir Francis Chichester, KBE; Mrs Sharon Sites Adams; Oliver J Lee and Peter K Poland (designer and builders of Hunters Boats); the editor and staff of *Yachting* (USA); the editor and staff of *Motor Boat and Yachting* and also *Yachting Monthly* (GB); Mrs Sheila P König of New Zealand; Vertue Owners Association; Mark Fishwick and John Mannering, *Yachting Monthly* correspondents; A H Moody & Son Ltd; Nicholas T Clifton of *Stardrift*; Albert Evans of Polynesian Catamarans; Jane A Yeoman of the *Sunday Express*; G R Cath (*Hunter 19*); Ray Webb; Gordon Gill; Charles Glass; Jean Taupin; Pat Patterson, Regional Director of the National Maritime Union of America in Japan; H Pilgrim; Patricia O'Driscoll of *East Coast Digest*; Joe Hines, Society of Spritsail Barge Research; the Senior Archivist of Ipswich and East Suffolk; Erick Manners, catamaran designer; Commander J P M Godber, RN(Ret.), Secretary of the Royal Naval Sailing Association; Kaoru Ogimi, Chief Executive Officer of the Nippon Ocean Racing Club; the directors of the Maritime Historical Association Inc. of Mystic, Connecticut; and the Maritime Museums of British Columbia, Victoria, and Hamburg; David Pardon, editor of *Sea Spray* (New Zealand); Charles and Susan Dennis of *Snoopy*; Major J J Dillon, Secretary of the Royal Yacht Squadron; The Defence and Naval Attache's Office, Italian Embassy, London; Shotaro Takahashi, Ambassador of Japan in Kuwait; Dan Holm, author of *The Circumnavigators*; Richard Henderson, author of *The Singlehanders*; Ursula Jupp, authority on Voss' voyages; the Royal Netherlands Embassy, London.

Contents

Illustrations

Collecting photographs of singlehanders is no easy matter. I am indebted to the following for their kind assistance in supplying prints and, where necessary, obtaining permission to publish.

Rupert Hart-Davis, publishers of *The Life and Voyages of Captain Joshua Slocum* by Victor Slocum.
The Director of the Maritime Museum of British Columbia in Victoria.
R G McCloskey, founder of the Slocum Society.
Mrs Sheila König
Bob Salmon
Erick J Manners, designer of World Cat.
Mrs Sharon Sites Adams, and photographer Werner Marhold of Huntington Beach, California.
Clare Francis
Andrzej Marczak of *Trybuna Ludu*
Nautical Publishing Company, publishers of *Capsize* by Bill King.
Norman C Cross of San Diego, trimaran designer.
Derek Messenger of Whangarei, New Zealand.
David Pardon, editor of *Sea Spray*.
Kaoru Ogimi, director of The Reader's Digest of Japan.
Sven A Hansson and the editor of *Pa Kryss & Till Rors* (photograph by Anders Skoot).

Adventure on, companion, for this
Is God's most greatest gift, the thing that is.
Take it, although it lead to the abyss.

Go forth to seek: the quarry never found
Is still a fever to the questing hound.
The skyline is a promise, not a bound.

Therefore, go forth, companion: when you find
No highway more, no track, all being blind
The way to go shall glimmer in the mind.

Though you have conquered Earth and charted Sea
And planned the courses of all Stars that be,
Adventure on, more wonders are in Thee.

Adventure on, for from the littlest clue
Has come whatever worth man ever knew;
The next to lighten all men may be you.

Adventure on, companion, the attempt
At high adventure brings reward undreamt.
The raging sea is grim with reefs unconn'd:
There is a way, a haven is beyond.
Way for yourself, a harbourage for you,
Where every quarry spirit can pursue
Is, in the glory of the dream come true.

from *The Ending* by John Masefield

Introduction

Like many other projects in which I have been involved, I drifted very slowly into this one, until the moment came when I realized that I was embayed—and very nearly on a lee shore. Throughout the years since 1934 I have been collecting facts about small boat adventures. In 1957, being jobless, my wife Mollie, our ten year old son Kester and I sailed our floating home—a 115 ton Thames sailing barge built in 1897 when she was named *John & Mary*— from Brigg in Lincolnshire to Mistley in Essex. With no engines, and a vast weight of gear alow and aloft, she was a challenge in more ways than one, yet we managed to complete the last long coasting voyage up towards the London River ever to be made by a motorless spritsail river barge with such a limited crew (*East Coast Passage*, Longmans 1971). It was not an easy task: I was at the helm for three days and two nights without a break. We had strong, adverse winds for most of the time—and one uneasy calm, which our flat-bottomed barge translated into rolling misery, for the winds which had all the time kept us pinned to a lee shore had created some nasty seas before they abated. *J & M* creaked in her sixty year old joints, and leaked—badly. One foot depth of bilge over the ceiling became three feet when the barge heeled. Mollie and Kester stacked carpets and furniture, but they were unable to save the heavy crate which contained my collection of small boat records and photographs, plus invaluable notes and over one thousand pictures of air-to-air and air-to-ground fighting which I had taken personally during World War II. My books, fortunately, were saved. Even then I had a collection of over two hundred about yacht voyaging.

When I introduced the first commercially successful trimarans into the UK, Europe and Africa in 1961, I had almost completely forgotten about my earlier interest in yacht cruising and small boat records. My customers, however, soon re-aroused my latent knowledge, for they took to tris like ducks to water, and many of them began in their own right to set up new 'firsts' and 'fastests'— though not necessarily in trimarans.

For example, Bill Nance, who subsequently sailed round the world in *Cardinal Vertue* via the Roaring Forties, wrote to me for advice from Africa where he was working far underground drilling for diamonds (a physically arduous job which he stuck for two years in order to finance his planned circumnavigation). After many letters, he arrived in England and proclaimed his willing- ness to learn about the sea, since he had no previous experience. I was able to introduce him to Bob Roberts, skipper of the last coasting barge in trade, *Cambria*, and Bill sailed in this 180 ton motorless ship for about six months before he bought his tiny yacht of only $4\frac{1}{2}$ tons displacement. The voyage, 1962–5, was largely ignored by the press, and yet until 1974 his was the smallest boat to go round by the southern route, and he was the first Australian ever to complete a solo circumnavigation.

In the meantime, trimarans which I had sold were beginning to break records too. Alex Grimes and Roy Garsides (British) sailed a Nimble class sloop ($30' \times 18' \times 2'$) from Wells, Norfolk to New Zealand (1962–3)—the first tri to cross two oceans. In 1964 Red Stolle (American) was the first trimaraner to cruise singlehanded across the Atlantic in his Victress class ketch ($40' \times 22' \times 2'9''$).

Chichester's much-publicized rounding of Cape Horn, and subsequent completion of the first circumnavigation with only one stopover, coincided with my leaving trimarans in 1966 and deciding to spend a few years in writing some books I had in mind. I knuckled down to my work, and still did not take overmuch notice of the small boat records which were being broken in rapid succession. It was not until 1969 when writing *The Lure of the Sea* that I began to revert to my early record collecting days. At the commencement of Chapter 2 I wrote: 'It always comes as a bit of a shock when I meet a blue-water escapist and discover he hasn't a clue about those who preceded him.' At this point I laid down my pen as the horrible truth dawned on me that although I remembered quite a bit about

15

pre-World War II voyages, I knew very little about post-war efforts. Chichester and Rose had been knighted by the Queen, the *Sunday Times* Golden Globe Race round the world singlehanded was still in progress, and yet here was I professing to know something about the game, although in fact I was very nearly as ignorant as the enthusiastic journalists who were proclaiming 'firsts' and 'fastests' for every triumphant arrival. Not only the journalists but sometimes the singlehanders themselves made claims which I was quite sure were incorrect.

I began to check. The *Guinness Book of Records*, I discovered, was decidedly canny in avoiding direct statements. I began by writing to them and putting a few facts right. Norris McWhirter was seemingly sufficiently interested in my knowledge to offer me the opportunity of writing a book on the subject. However, I knew from past experience that collecting material of this nature is very nearly an impossible task, and although I was perfectly prepared to help somebody else, I didn't want to get saddled with the job myself. Besides—silly fool!—I wanted to write a novel.

I wrote my novel. It was now mid-summer 1973. Over the past three years I had collected quite a wad of information about small boat records. 'Why not try to list just the solo circumnavigators?' I asked myself. So I spread a clean sheet of foolscap folio on my desk and wrote: (1) Joshua Slocum, *Spray*. I knew Josh was born in Nova Scotia, but I couldn't remember the exact dimensions of his boat. I looked them up in his book. At the same time I made a note of the years . . .

The list began to lengthen . . . Soon, there were two lists . . . three . . .

I started to write letters then, to try to fill in gaps. To my horror nobody else seemed to know very much about the subject either, and it was not very long before *I* was being asked to solve yacht record claims based on the flimsiest of evidence obtained by me (or supplied by them). The only two modern books which give useful information are *Atlantic Adventurers*** by Humphrey Barton, and *Sea Quest* by Charles A Borden, but although excellent in many respects they certainly do not supply enough details for the positive identification of 'firsts' and 'fastests' or other yachting milestones.

I have done my best in this first-ever small boat record book to sort out and distinguish the many varieties of singlehanded

*Books mentioned by title only are listed more fully in the Bibliography.

voyages. In order to give some perspective to the modern solo adventures at sea, it is necessary to go back to earlier voyages, for the commanders of those exploratory ships must have been even more singleminded in purpose than the present-day blue-water adventurers to persist against the impossible odds which they faced, and as will be seen some of the earliest solo 'firsts' were inextricably linked with those voyages.

Although I have been most careful, there are bound to be mistakes and anomalies in this book. For example, I have in front of me two photographs of Vito Dumas' round-the-world yacht *Legh II*—or that is how it is spelt in one photo; the other clearly shows *Lehg II*. I ask you, how can one possibly be *accurate* with such conflicting evidence?

So I can only add this. If *you* know something, or have a photograph, or if I can help *you* to solve a record problem, then please write to me and help me to ensure that in due course every small boat record-breaker receives some credit. Many are modest and do not want recognition, but on the other hand it must be obvious that for too many years this part of yachting history has been almost forgotten because nobody has bothered to collate the facts. I have done my best this time, but the final result is in your hands. If you really want to know the truth, the whole truth and nothing but the truth then *you* will have to supply it!

'Gables'
Woolverstone
Ipswich, Suffolk IP9 1BA
England

1
The Early Voyages

In the beginning there must have been some lonely soul who departed on a short voyage from A to B and finished up at Z—to become the first long distance singlehander. Such events continue to happen to this day, and surprisingly, voyages in this class can still break records.

On February 2, 1964 a flat-bottomed dinghy left Maupiti for Bora Bora, only a few miles away, carrying goods for sale in the market there. On board were Tahitians Demanihi Tepa (aged thirty) and Natua Faloho (forty). A mile or so offshore their outboard broke down and they were unable to restart it. With no oars, paddles, sails or tools on board, their small boat immediately began to drift rapidly, driven by the Trade Winds and the powerful current away from land and out into the vastness of the Pacific. On July 6, 155 days and 1400 miles later, the boat came ashore at Tau Island (70 miles east of Pago) with the sole survivor, the younger man Tepa, still alive. He told how they had caught fish with an improvised spear made from an old scissor blade and a strip of wood torn from the boat, how tropical rain showers had given them water, how his companion had died after 141 days. Tepa lost 70 lbs during this drift, the longest period ever sustained by a person starting off with little or no supplies.

Even more remarkable, because he was entirely alone from the beginning, was the 133 day drift on an unstocked Carley Float (raft) made by Second Steward Poon Lim, whose ship *Ben Lomond* was torpedoed some 750 miles off the Azores on November 23, 1942. This hardy, Hong Kong-born, British merchant seaman was rescued off Salinas, Brazil on April 5, 1943 and amazingly he was in sufficiently fit condition to be able to walk ashore. He told how he had extracted nails from the raft to make fishhooks, unravelled some of his clothing to make lines, and collected precious rain water. The event was considered of enough importance at the time to describe to us fighter pilots, who had only an unstocked K-type dinghy on which to rely if we happened to get shot down in the drink. We did point out that the inflatable cushion of our seat-type parachute precluded the use of nails, so a small tin box containing two fishhooks and other bits and pieces was squeezed into the dinghy pack. They gave Poon Lim a BEM—and they condemned us to sore backsides. I have yet to meet a pilot who succeeded in catching a fish from a K-type dinghy with the survival kit supplied by the RAF.

From such records as these we can deduce that somebody had to be the first to suffer the awful experience—somewhere. But we don't know who. One thing *is* certain, however, and that is that men were crossing oceans long before Christopher Columbus.

I am no scholar, and therefore I have to rely on the researches of those fortunate people who are able to translate the (to me) unpronounceable and frequently unreadable manuscripts which have been preserved in so many archives throughout the world. What secrets there must be in these ancient, tatty documents, so many still unread and others scarcely considered even when laboriously turned into the modern idiom. Yet I felt it was necessary to examine something of what happened before Columbus. Surely, *these* were the men who begat singlehanders?

The Vikings perhaps? But no, there was much going on in the Atlantic before then.

The earliest recorded transatlantic crossing was made by an Irishman, Brendan—afterwards termed the Navigator, and later still sainted, though I doubt if this was for his astonishing voyages. In a most carefully researched book *Brendan the Navigator* (published in Ireland by M H Gill & Son, 1945) Dr George A Little describes in detail the almost unbelievable adventures of this Irish monk who reached the American continent some 433 years before the first Viking (Eric Rauda—the Red), and 940 years before Columbus.

Brendan's initial voyage of exploration resulted from a story told to him by his kinsman and religious confidant, Fionn-Barr of Ardfert. A monk who had once lived in his house, one Mernoc, had fled secretly to sea in order to find greater piety in the solitude

19

of some rocky island, where whatever miniscule bodily comforts he had weakly allowed himself on the mainland would be reduced almost literally to bare survival, and thereby (presumably) to greater holiness. In due course Fionn-Barr decided to find Mernoc, and after three days met him cruising at sea. Sailing together for a further three days, eventually they made Mernoc's island where, by this time, several monks had set up a community. For many days Fionn-Barr and Mernoc together explored this island. Then Mernoc admitted to knowing of a wonderful country, too magnificent to describe, which he wished to show his friend. They provisioned a boat and set forth, and in due course landed on the shores of an incredible place which, from their description, was no worse than Paradise. This they explored for a long time, until they came to a great river. Here it was revealed to them that the time was not right for them to stay, and that they must return from whence they came. Sadly, they obeyed.

Needless to say, on hearing this story Brendan immediately seized the opportunity of facing danger and hardship in order to rediscover this Paradise. He was not interested in milk and honey, for his austere mind could only consider such pleasures if they acted as a stimulant to his devotions, but the frightful task of endeavour certainly made the prospect desirable, so he consulted his religious companions. They liked the idea so much that they volunteered as crew.

Brendan's first voyage in a giant curragh, with a total crew of fourteen, is of interest mainly because it demonstrates that protracted passages in small boats were being accomplished from the British Isles long before the time historians generally give. Curraghs (and the similar Eskimo *umiak*) are still used occasionally to this day, but they were extremely popular in Irish fishing communities until the earlier part of the twentieth century because the design makes such a wonderful sea boat, and because the craft is comparatively easy and cheap to build.

Brendan's curragh had some interesting features. The ribs and gunwales were of willow, with the interstices filled with wicker. The skeleton frame was covered with three layers of oak-tanned hides, arranged to form two air chambers. Joints in the hides were sealed with holly resin, and the whole tar caulked. The hides were kept supple and waterproof with butter, as was the triangular leather lugsail which was carried on a short mast stepped in the forward part of the vessel. Long sweeps supplied propulsion, and some lateral balance if needed. Fire was carried in a charcoal brazier, mounted on two metal rods slung athwartships to keep the heat from the inflammable hull.

In AD 545 Brendan set sail from Kerry, and during the next five years visited St Kilda, the Faroes, the Shetlands and Iceland— and quartered the northern part of the Atlantic for as much as three months at a time in an attempt to locate Fionn-Barr's mysterious country. How they survived the weather and the seas in an open boat for so long is difficult to imagine—many times they very nearly failed—but hardship was what they sought, and they certainly found it in plenty. Brendan was sixty-six years old when he returned from this first-ever recorded ocean exploration.

A year later, in 551, he decided to make a second attempt to locate Fionn-Barr's land of plenty. This time he did not make his earlier theological error of leaving the navigation to the vagaries of wind and sea (i.e. to Fate). We do not know exactly how he navigated, but it is apparent that he used a *rutter* or sailing guide written by an experienced seaman who, possibly, had sailed westwards before.

His ship was built of oak, possibly decked all over, but more likely only decked forward and aft. She was in size and dimensions rather similar to a small Humber keel (a box-like, double ended vessel which used to trade on the River Humber until quite recently), and like the keel she carried a single woven squaresail on a mast stepped amidships. Surprisingly, no oars were shipped. There was a good deal of ironwork in her hull, including a large anchor with wrought chain; she was steered by a flexibly mounted oar over the starboard quarter. In this vessel, probably no bigger than about 50 ft overall, Brendan and his crew set forth, inspired by their religious beliefs and the proven seamanship of their leader.

If the recensions are to be believed, he was a remarkably well informed captain. It is claimed that among the stores and victuals loaded on board *An Trinóit* (as she may have been named, since she was dedicated to the Trinity), was a stock of the roots of blue sea-holly (*eryngium*) which he believed would safeguard the crew against scurvy. Certainly at a later date (fifteenth century) the anti-scorbutic quality of the roots was known. He shipped seeds, plants, live swine, dried fish, spare iron, tools, fire, and many casks and water skins. Since he had no compass or lodestone, he also took three trained ravens which he could release one at a time when he believed he was near land. (One wonders whether he obtained this idea from the biblical story of Noah.) He even signed a jester, one Crosan, anticipating a much later practice of having a chantyman on virtually all sailing ships.

In March, AD 551, all being well, Brendan and his crew prayed, then weighed anchor and set forth into the semi-unknown from the roadstead east of Aran Mór in County Mayo.

Forty days later, they found themselves in a region of gloom, fog and icebergs—almost certainly the Grand Banks. Shortly after, they discovered the rocky coast of Newfoundland but did not land as they were uncertain of the temper of the many walrus which they found there; they coasted southwards. Crosan, popular with everybody, died; he was buried ashore in an unnamed bay. Next, the smith died—we are not told of what—in the region of Cape Race. Brendan did not wish to land, since they were well offshore, so he ordered that the body should be buried at sea.

Eventually they fetched up at the Bahamas, possibly Abaco, where they discovered a hostile race who were probably the Arawaks (subsequently exterminated by the Caribs). Brendan would not allow his men ashore, although his ship was anchored here for seven days, for, he said, should they do so 'they would be forced to fight—and to spill human blood was not their business'. Unfortunately, when they tried to leave the lagoon the anchor fouled and they were forced to abandon it. Without smith or anchor, Brendan sailed to Grand Bahama Island.

Here, incredibly, they found an oratory—and an ancient man, greatly emaciated. He claimed he was Irish, and that his community had once numbered twelve. Brendan arrived just in time to bestow the last sacraments, for shortly afterwards the old man died. The ship then departed from this unhappy place.

Next they landed in the area of Florida now called Miami. Here, for the first time, Brendan and his crew believed they had reached the target of their long voyage. They saw 'a land odorous, flower-smooth, blessed; a land many-melodied, musical, shouting for joy, unmournful'. Here was the place to moor their vessel awhile and explore the interior.

They were amazed to discover yet another old man, an Irish monk by the name of Festivus who claimed to have been there for some thirty years, since 522. After long discussions with this man, Brendan set off on an exploration of the interior of Florida which was to last about forty days. Surprisingly accurately, following Fionn-Barr's original description, they came to a wide river which they were unable to cross (possibly St Johns River in Florida, or even the Mississippi has been suggested). Here they met up with a very handsome young man (a Shawanee Indian?) who persuaded the men to return to their base camp. This they did, to spend many days at prayer in company with Festivus at their original landing site. Here, as time passed, they were joined by members of yet another mission who, at some unspecified period, had preceded them into Florida, and about whom, unfortunately, no records appear to exist.

But now, having accomplished what he had set out to do, and having discovered that other Christians had already established a religious bridgehead, as it were, Brendan sought the advice of Festivus. We do not know what passed between them, but the result was that the Navigator decided to return to Ireland. In seven years' voyaging he had discovered Irish monks scattered all around the fringes of the North Atlantic, most of them living under appalling conditions. Now he could return with a message of hope to the many pagans and sinners who were still plentiful enough in his own country.

They returned via the Grand Banks to Aran Mór, and after a month's rest there sailed to an island (now called Coney) 'in the quiet waters of the Shannon estuary at the point of its confluence with the River Fergus, abreast of the town of Ennis'. Here they again prayed and fasted, and here two more of his crew died (no doubt as a result of all the hardships which they had endured). In due course, it was here that Brendan built a monastery.

At the completion of his second voyage, he was nearly seventy. That he went on yet another adventurous exploration, partly by sea but much of it overland, does not concern us here, though perhaps it is interesting to note that this incredible man died on May 16, 577 at the age of ninety-three, and was buried at Clonfert in County Galway.

In his book Dr Little gives more than adequate proof that these two amazing voyages were not just figments of Irish imagination. Old Brendan made his landfalls, just as surely as Eric the Red made Cape Cod, Narragansett Bay and Rhode Island in AD 985, and his son, Lief Erikson lived in Vinland for a whole year in 1002. The thirteenth century Eyrbyggia Saga survives to spell it out, and mentions too how one Gudlief, a merchant, trading from Dublin to Iceland in 939 was blown off course to fetch up on an unknown shore (established as Newfoundland) where the people spoke to him in Irish. No doubt disbelievers will continue to scoff, but I for one support Dr Little's contention that Brendan the Navigator qualified for a surprising number of 'firsts' in transocean crossings, including the first-ever recorded transatlantic passage.*

You may well ask, what has this got to do with singlehanders? The answer is that since we are at the beginning of this investigation it is as well to consider those who first accomplished voyages of any sort, for did we not learn everything we know as a result of their efforts? Consider the two long drifts mentioned earlier in this chapter. It has long been known that the Polynesians were sailing around the Pacific Ocean—and navigating accurately by a variety of methods—at a time when Western Europeans were living in fear and much squalor. Surely, two thousand years or so of making long sea passages in small boats must have ingrained some form of marine survival ability into the mind of Demanihi Tepa? Similarly with Poon Lim, born in that hive of manmade poverty, Hong Kong; perhaps he lacked the Polynesian affinity for water, but certainly with his background he did not have to be taught how to find food in order to survive.

But these were merely involuntary voyages. Think of Brendan as a singlehander, and I submit that all the leaders of early sea voyages must have been singlehanders at heart, up to and including most of the first circumnavigators. Born into the royal blood of Niall, educated under the auspices of Bishop Erc (an ex-Druid turned Christian), Brendan most decidedly was not the innocent, simple man of piety which one might inadvertently assume of monks of nearly 1500 years ago. He was proficient in several languages, top of his class in geometry and mathematics, well versed in astronomy, and had the Irish gift of poetry and music. He learned much of herbalism and natural philosophy, and from Erc no doubt he discovered a great deal about the mysteries of the Druidical culture, in which the movements and manifestations of celestial bodies were an integral part. In addition, he had been thoroughly indoctrinated in the belief that not only was manual labour an essential method of subduing the flesh, but that

---

*In 1966 Bill Verity of Fenit, County Kerry, Ireland retraced Brendan's return voyage in a specially designed 12 ft boat which, although small, was extremely well equipped. In 1969 he built a 20 ft replica of Brendan's transatlantic vessel which he named *Noamh Breandan*; she was rigged with a squaresail and steered by a stern oar exactly as the original. Verity left Fenit on May 23, 1969 and after a long and difficult passage finally arrived at San Salvador (or Watling Island) in the Bahamas, very near Brendan's assumed landfall. This extremely good effort does not necessarily prove the authenticity of Brendan's voyage—which is a matter for archaeologists—but it is well worth recording as being somewhat different to the more usual raft emigration theories.

it was also necessary to implement the vow of poverty, which demanded that whoever had taken it must perform such chores as to yield sustenance, not only for himself but for the destitute as well. His life was thus decreed as one of ceaseless learning, labour and hard living.

It is not surprising, therefore, that even in his youth he had no time for women. It is told that a girl from his village once tried to make advances, and that he 'drove her from him with harsh, impetuous anger'. This trait is not exclusive to Brendan, and can be discovered behind the scenes of many a singlehander's life.

So we begin to see a pattern of a man who, although he did not sail alone, had all the basic requirements of a loner. He was thoroughly versed in self-discipline. He was of above-average intelligence and a capable navigator (though his methods are lost to us). His dedication to his religion ensured that he would always be philosophical whenever things went wrong, and that he would never whine for help from others more 'fortunate' than himself. He was tough, both physically and mentally: he was a leader of men, not an escaper of men and responsibilities. And he was a seaman, taught by fishermen in the stormy seas off the Atlantic-facing west Irish coast; he was also a jack-of-all-trades, an essential craft for every monk (and seaman). Above all, he was religiously dedicated, but not to the selfish extent of ignoring everything but his own religion; that he wanted to explore, to find other lands at the expense of his own flesh, is proof enough of this.

If I must fault him—and I feel I should—it is because he apparently left no personal records of his voyages. All too often loners, through modesty, desire of privacy or just damned laziness, shun putting pen to paper. I am in no doubt that Brendan's reason was none of these—that in fact he merely regarded his voyages as a defense against religious stagnation—in other words, to save himself from becoming a religious cabbage. Prolonged solitude, particularly under the harsh rules of the religious fanaticism of those early Christian days, evolved some queer fancies.

It would be nice to read what Brendan himself thought about this and that, instead of getting it secondhand from an Irish storyteller who, for all I know, may never have been to sea. One has only to read a journalist's account of something in which one has been personally involved to understand that secondhand stories bear little resemblance to the truth.

On this score, I entirely agree with Weston Martyr (a trans-ocean yachtsman of the 1920s and 30s, but not a singlehander), who began his book *The Wandering Years* (Blackwood, 1940) with this criticism. 'Men should tell what they know. If my father had told me, at fifteen, a little of what he knew at fifty-five, he would have saved me a world of trouble and grief. He died, aged ninety-two, and he took all he knew with him. Remembering his career, I feel he must have known a lot.'

Singlehanders could have learned much from Brendan.

But we must leave him to consider some of the other early sea voyagers. The Vikings and Columbus are too well known (and grossly over-popularized) to investigate here, and I haven't read enough about the early Chinese junk or Arab dhow explorations to comment. After Columbus the Portuguese, Vasco da Gama, made a remarkable passage to India via the Cape of Good Hope (1497–9), but in my opinion Ferdinand Magellan (actually, Magalhães), who dared to consider a voyage around the world, is of more interest to us because he opened a gateway to the Pacific which the Spanish did not realize existed, and thereby proved by example what had been known for many centuries—that the world was indeed round. Nine hundred and sixty-six years had passed since Brendan rediscovered America, yet Magellan was the first to conceive and lead (but, alas, not to achieve himself) a circumnavigation.

It is interesting to consider how little we would have known about this voyage if the Italian scholar Antonio Pigafetta had not been excited by Magellan's imaginative scheme to the extent that he asked to be allowed to join the expedition. If Magellan had refused, we would know almost nothing about this great adventure, apart from some navigational details remaining in the log of Francesco Albo, a surviving pilot of the Spanish Armada, who was also one of the eighteen survivors of this first circumnavigation. As it is, Pigafetta recorded everything that happened during the eventful years 1519–22.

Although Fate was kind in this respect, Magellan was as dedicated to his dream as Brendan had been, and it was his purposefulness which achieved results. Having returned to Lisbon after seven years' exploration around India and the Moluccas, he first presented his plan for a circumnavigation to the Portuguese authorities. When they turned him down, he immediately moved to Spain, changed his nationality, married a

Spanish woman and set about persuading King Charles I (who was then only seventeen) into taking an interest in his venture. How can such determination fail? Fortunately for Magellan, the King and some wealthy merchants agreed to support his venture, but I have no doubt that a flat refusal would merely have meant further nationality-swapping, and perhaps wife-changing as well, before he obtained the support he needed. (This trait of single-mindedness can be found to this day in many successful singlehanders.)

It is not my intention to describe voyages which are already well known. Wind and sea, the great wilderness which exists between continents, is the same today as it was then—apart, perhaps, from the creeping death of pollution which permeates everywhere. Take yourself into that loneliness by boat, out of sight of land, and you will experience hopes and fears not all that different from Brendan's and Magellan's, though much will depend on how much you know, how well you are provisioned and equipped, and the type of vessel you are on. If you are ignorant of the ways of a ship upon the sea, and you have no food or water, and your boat is rotten and leaky—then your fears will be infinitely greater than those of the early navigators who, in spite of the sea monsters and devils inscribed on their charts, were not simpletons. They knew precisely what they were up against as far as wind and weather were concerned, and they were armed with guns and their religious beliefs against any unknown opposition.

You can read all about these early voyages if you are interested enough to make the effort, but unless you are an extremely experienced seaman you will not be able to read between the lines. In this investigation of singlehanders, therefore, I prefer to draw your attention to those features which normally you would not notice, rather than repeat the hackneyed details of the voyages which are all so very similar.

Think, for example, of the five ships which Magellan chose for his fleet: Flagship *Trinidada* (110 tons burthen), *San Antonio* (120 tons), *Concepcion* (90 tons), *Vittoria* (85 tons) and *Santiago* (75 tons). The Flagship's dimensions have been worked out as being 78' × 22'6" × 8' draft; she could carry fifty-five people. My Thames sailing barge measured 81' × 18' × 3', and was mostly sailed (she was without an engine) by Mollie, Kester and myself. The largest *singlehanded* yachts to circumnavigate have been Chay Blyth's *British Steel* (59' × 12'10" × 8') and Tom Blackwell's

Islander (58′6″ × 12′8″ × 7′8″). When is a ship not a ship? When it
becomes a small boat in order to break records?

We are not really concerned with the hazards which Magellan
faced during the voyage. I have introduced him into this book to
point out his imaginative singlemindedness, and to compare the
size of his craft with those of his singlehanded imitators some 450
years later. It is also interesting to note that the period between
Brendan's and Magellan's voyages is slightly more than double
the years between Magellan's and the circumnavigations of
modern yachts: 966 years, then about 450 years. I wonder what
the small boat adventurer will be doing, and sailing, in say the
year 2200?

So Magellan crossed the Pacific, which he named for the peace
it gave him after the horrors he had experienced getting there, but
his religious zeal was not tempered with the sound commonsense
which Brendan displayed in the Bahamas. The 'heathen savages'
of Mactan objected to his attempts at conversion, and killed him
on April 27, 1521. *Santiago* had been lost on the Patagonian
coast, *San Antonio* had sailed for home with the news that
Magellan and the rest of the fleet had been lost among the
whirlpools and tidal races of his Strait; now the worm-riddled,
worn out *Concepcion* was burned and *Trinidada* was sent back
across the Pacific to Mexico (she failed to make it). The little
Vittoria, captained by Sebastian del Cano, completed the voyage
around the world with a hold stuffed full of cloves and many
other spices—more than sufficient to pay for all the losses, but at
the additional appalling cost of mutiny, blackmail, double dealing,
murder, incredible privations and miserable deaths, all of which,
naturally, were blamed on Magellan. His heirs were forgotten,
and his Spanish wife Dona Beatriz died of a broken heart; but
Captain del Cano reaped every possible honour and award, and
became the hero of the voyage. Nobody bothered to recall that he
had at one stage joined the mutineers who had caused Magellan
so much trouble. But these days we say 'that's life', and shrug
our shoulders and dash out to greet the current nine-day-wonder,
just as we are meant to do.

Pigafetta, though, at least gave more to mankind than a fleeting
fat profit. Afterwards he wrote:

> Leaving Seville, I went to Valladolid, where I presented to
> his Sacred Majesty Don Carlos neither gold nor silver, but

things much more precious in the eyes of so great a Sovereign. I presented to him among other things a book written by my hand of all the things that had occurred day by day in our voyage. I departed thence as I was best able and went to Portugal, and related to King John the things I had seen. Returning to Spain, I came to France, where I presented a few things from the other hemisphere to Madam the Regent, mother of the most Christian King Don Francis. Afterwards I returned to Italy, where I established forever my abode, and devoted my leisure and vigil to the very illustrious and noble Phillip de Villiers Lisleaden, the very worthy Master of Rhodes.

So Pigafetta, too, did very well as a result of his efforts, and in due course was appointed a Knight of Rhodes. Only Ferdinand Magellan, his wife and his children received nothing but ignominious death: an unhappiness which all too often is the sole reward some still receive to this day for their achievements at sea—a few of which I will describe in due course.

In the beginning, then, small boats set forth to cross oceans out of two motives: religion and reward. For the most part both were inextricably combined, although I doubt whether Brendan thought very much about the latter. Joshua Slocum set forth to sail alone around the world because 'the wonderful sea charmed me from the first', and apparently for no other reason (even although his shrewd trading ability ensured an occasional profit, and he was afterwards a determined salesman of his famous book).

If Brendan failed to convince anybody that crossing the Atlantic was well worth further consideration, Pigafetta's report certainly prompted action. In 1525 the Spanish sent a powerful armada of seven ships to exploit Magellan's discoveries, under the command of Gracia Jofre de Loaysa. The Flagship *Santa Maria de la Vittoria*, a mighty vessel of 300 tons burthen, got through the Strait of Magellan but was sunk at Tidore in the East Indies. All the other ships either were wrecked, deserted the fleet, or were lost after interminable fighting with the Portuguese. In spite of this failure, however, others soon followed, and who can say how many lonely voyages were accomplished by those who were shipwrecked or marooned, or lost overboard, or who were just plain deserters from the brutalities and hardships of shipboard life? It is known that many of them eventually drifted back to their homeland after many years' absence. Seldom are we told how they made it.

So the recent 'drifting' records which I mentioned at the beginning of this chapter are not necessarily correct for all time, and I suspect that in this early period many 'records' were set up. The Spanish and the Portuguese had ruled the seas since 1492: around eighty years had to pass before the British challenged them for the rewards of ocean exploration, thereby opening up a new potential for small boat record-breaking.

2
Introduction to Sponsorship

Sponsorship is an ugly word which, unfortunately, is currently becoming an adjunct to many singlehanded projects. Someone has to pay for the boat, its equipment, the fitting out and the attempt, whatever it may be, since the average loner just does not have that sort of money. This implies that virtually all modern sponsored voyages can be regarded as being for reward, because the person aboard the boat is committed by the financial interest of others to do his utmost to achieve success. Sponsor comes from a Latin word which means 'to promise'—a two-edged implication. Thus our sponsored singlehander is no longer a true yachtsman, since such a person sails only *for pleasure or sport*. This point should have been considered when 'exceptional yachtsman' awards have been given for fully or part sponsored record voyages.

Of course sponsorship is not new. Most of the early transocean explorers operated under the auspices of a patron or investors. Magellan had his King and some wealthy merchants—one of whom, Christopher Haro of Seville, put up a fifth of the total cost, and subsequently received nothing back. The overall investment of the five ships, complete with guns and appurtenances, provisions, trade goods, plus four months' advance pay for 237 people, came to 8·76 million maravedis, so obviously Magellan had to rely on backers.

Drake, the second successful circumnavigator and the first to do so in the ship in which he set out, was in a somewhat different situation. Drake had already collected a sizeable fortune from his

31

famous voyage against Spain in the 200 ton *Swan*, during which he sacked the town of Nombre de Dios and took an enormous treasure. He had also climbed a mountain on the Isthmus of Panama, and from the upper branches of a tree had seen the Pacific. Being a glory-seeker, with a natural bent for public relations (he deliberately brought his ships into Plymouth on a Sunday when everybody was at church; he then ensured that his arrival would never be forgotten by firing his guns and hauling aloft his victory pennants: the pious townsfolk, needless to say, promptly deserted the churches for the more immediate pleasures of hero-worship—and possible gain from the two treasure-stuffed ships), Drake first made himself very popular with his Queen before submitting the plan he had evolved as a result of this experience.

Elizabeth I was noted both for her meanness and her patriotism. At his own expense (or rather the Spaniards'), Drake fitted out three frigates and cruised the coasts of Erin to help subdue the rebellious Irish. His Queen was delighted with this gift. Only then did he put up his proposition of a treasure-seeking voyage in the Pacific, and subsequent avoidance of angry Spaniards by sailing on round the world, pointing out that most of Spain's gold and silver originated from the coasts of Chile and Peru. He ensured that he was the principal shareholder, but he allowed selected friends to contribute and made quite a show of the substantial financial interest taken by the Crown. Naturally the Queen promoted him from being merely a successful privateer by giving him a Commission. So Captain-General Francis Drake departed with just about every ace in the pack firmly tucked up his sleeve. 'We doe account,' Elizabeth had told him, 'that he who striketh at thee, striketh at us.'

His Flagship *Pelican* (later re-named *Golden Hind*) was about the same size as Magellan's Flagship *Trinidada*; the rest of his fleet were much smaller. One hundred and sixty-three 'gentlemen and sailors' crewed the five ships—unpaid, unless they won every battle against the Spaniards, nature, and just about anybody or anything else they might meet on the voyage.

Drake took his ship safely through the Magellan Straits and then ran into some terrible weather shortly after he entered the South Sea. Driven southwestwards, he found and named Elizabeth Island, now the submerged Burnam Bank, and there landed to collect food and water. As far as is known, Drake and a few of his men were the only people ever to have visited this

32

uninhabited island before it disappeared forever, undoubtedly in one of the violent oceanic 'quakes which to this day continue to breed or swallow islands. For a long time afterwards Drake was credited with discovering and landing on the southernmost island tip of the South American continent (later named Cape Horn), which is actually 250 miles or so to the east of the position of Drake's Elizabeth Island.

I mention this fact because it demonstrates how easily a popular misconception can arise, and how difficult it is to erase a myth once it has been established. To test this statement, I asked a mixed gurgle of lunchtime drinkers in my local pub 'Who discovered Cape Horn? Who was the first Englishman to round Cape Horn?' The answers were varied (it *was* a pub), but the general consensus was that Drake both discovered and sailed round the Horn. 'Wasn't it a Dutchman called Horn who actually named it?' somebody suggested. 'No, he called it after his home town, but Drake was there first,' somebody else recalled.

In fact, the first British captain to round Cape Horn was the pirate Bartholomew Sharp who, on his way home from a reasonably successful series of raids on Spanish towns, after crossing the Isthmus of Panama on foot and capturing some large Spanish ships in which to fight, rounded eastabout, having missed the entrance to the Magellan Straits in foul weather, on November 15, 1681. This was just over a century after Drake was in those waters, and sixty-five after a Dutchman, Willem Cornelis Schouten, had discovered and rounded Cape Horn westabout on January 29, 1616. It is said that in a fading twilight Schouten thought only of home, and cried 'Cape Hoorn! Cape Hoorn!' after his beloved town. I feel it is more reasonable to suspect that the 110 ton *Hoorn*, which accompanied the 360 ton Flagship *Een-dracht*, was honoured on this occasion. She carried only twenty-two crew, against sixty-five in the Flagship, and I would prefer to think that tough but kindly Willem thought more of his men at a time like this than he did of his home town.

Schouten was an exceptional navigator and captain. In all his subsequent wanderings across the Pacific, during which he traded fairly and profitably, he treated both his crew and any captives with kindness and humanity. Finally, deeply laden with valuable goods, he fetched up in the Dutch East India Company's harbour of Bantam. During the long passage he had lost only one man: the carpenter's mate, who died of natural causes just before they reached Madeira.

Yet this great voyage of discovery was immediately condemned by the big business interests of the day: in brief, the Eastern Council of the Company attacked poor Schouten for lying. A new strait south of Magellan, an area known to be closely guarded by Spaniards, who were so jealous of their properties in the great South Sea? Ridiculous! These two ships were guilty of stealing from the Dutch East India Company. They would be confiscated! Schouten was sent home in disgrace, in steerage, on board the Company's *Amsterdam*, and in this manner he completed his circumnavigation.

It is true that two years after his return, when his and his supercargo's narratives of the first rounding of Cape Hoorn were published, and a Dutch court had ordered the greedy East India Company to pay back the value of everything they had stolen, Willem Schouten's honour was restored. Yet he had had to fight hard, and unnecessarily, against an arrogant and grasping commercial power.

Unfortunately I do not have the space to continue about these incredible men who conceived and achieved voyages against such appalling odds, which so often included their own countrymen. Although they sailed in ships mostly rammed tight with crews, they were, I'm sure, basically singlehanders in outlook, for even if they were naturally gregarious, as commanders they had little choice of mixing. A captain, whatever his rank on shore, was just one step short of God when he was at sea, and probably he was very nearly as lonely as any solo yachtsman. Undoubtedly he had far greater problems than the modern loner, for he had to contain his crew, maintain his ships and retain his sponsored purpose to produce a fat profit. One wonders why so many tried.

The pirates, on the other hand, had a much easier task. Frequently the captains were very nearly as ignorant about navigation and business matters as their crews. Without putting too fine an edge on it, Drake as a privateer was really no more than a licensed pirate; only his unusually clever self-promotion enabled him to steer clear of much of the political intrigue which went on behind the scenes at Court—and elsewhere. Often, even Drake very nearly succumbed. However, though he may have been a ruthless opponent, he was a first class navigator and seaman. Some pirates weren't even good seamen!

British privateering dates back to the thirteenth century, and piracy to the beginning of maritime history. Privateers cost the Crown nothing, and were a source of revenue and fighting

34

tonnage at all times, during both war and peace—the Crown naturally taking a proportion of the profits. Piracy, particularly in Elizabeth's time was controlled by a remarkable network of big syndicates, financed and directed by Lords Lieutenants, Sheriffs, high naval officers and government and civil service officials. These organizers did not take part in the actual sea fighting—once again the concept of sponsorship creeps in—but they handled the bribes, financing and other behind the scenes business to ensure that their ships, captains and crews had regular work and no worries. As investors they took four-fifths of any plunder, leaving one-fifth for the captain and crew to share between them. It was marvellously profitable. Plymouth, Southampton and many smaller ports were controlled by one or other of these big syndicates.

Elizabeth had some qualms before she knighted Drake at Deptford after his circumnavigation, which had ended on September 16, 1580. It was not until the following April that she spoke the words 'Arise, Sir Francis'. Lord Burleigh, and many other powerful opponents, had condemned Drake on both political and moral grounds, but Elizabeth had learned that her hero (or villain) had brought back at least £1·5 million value of booty, and this was an overpowering argument in his favour. Nearly forty years later, Sir Walter Raleigh was to fail to produce such persuasive evidence of his loyalty to his King after an equally important voyage, and so he lost his head. Modern sponsorship is not quite so demanding.

Nevertheless piracy and privateering gave men an opportunity to make something of their lives, and a great many freely chose the life in preference to hideous mediocrity ashore with little or no hope of ever bettering oneself, or the unsparing rigid discipline afloat in the Royal Navy and Merchant Service. The most daring of all pirates, Bartholomew Roberts, summed it up neatly when he remarked 'In an honest service there is thin commons, low wages and hard labour; but in a pirate life there is plenty and satiety, pleasure and ease, liberty and power.' Captain Charles Johnson, who in 1724 published *A General History of the Robberies and Murders of the Most Notorious Pyrates*, attributed the following to a pirate captain named Bellamy, who had just tried, without success, to convert the captain and crew of a prize he had taken to serve under the Black Flag.

Damn ye, you are a sneaking puppy, and so are all those who submit to be governed by laws which rich men have

35

made for their own security, for the cowardly whelps have not the courage otherwise to defend what they get by their knavery. Damn them for a pack of crafty rascals, and you who serve them for a parcel of hen-hearted numbskulls. They vilify us, the scoundrels do, when there is only this difference: they rob the poor under the cover of the law, forsooth, and we plunder the rich under the protection of our own courage. Had ye not better make one of us, than sneak after the arses of those villains for employment?

Captain Roberts was undoubtedly exaggerating the benefits of piracy, and his brief remark bears little resemblance to contemporary truth; but Captain Bellamy went on to castigate the reluctant merchant captain with all the wit of a modern communist agitator.

You are a devilish conscious rascal, damn ye! I am a free prince and have as much authority to make war on the whole world as he who has a hundred sail of ships and an army of a hundred thousand in the field; and this my conscience tells me. But there is no arguing with such snivelling puppies who allow superiors to kick them about deck for pleasure, and pin their faith upon a pimp of a parson—a squab who neither practices nor believes what he puts upon the chuckle-headed fools he preaches to.

Undoubtedly Bellamy was a freebooter, controlled by neither patron nor sponsors. I have read very similar philosophies in a few modern books written by anti-establishment single-handers, and in every case they too relied entirely upon their own wit and resource. The genuine loner would not have it ~~Undoubtedly Bellamy was a freebooter, controlled by neither~~ appreciate an audience to whom he could decry with as much ~~in a few modern books written by anti-establishment single-~~ between such piratically-minded singlehanders—the freebooters of modern yachtsmen—and the sponsored professionals: the latter get most of the publicity, and thereby all the writing space and air time; the former cut a lonely furrow, and nobody ever hears about them. Drake? Yes. Brendan? No. Sponsors tend to ensure that their heroes will remain in the public eye for as long as possible, and therefore reduce the chances of those who may have done better from getting due credit.

In this respect, with one particular promoter of a singlehanded voyage, who was actually proclaiming 'firsts' even before the feat was completed, I protested that others had done this and that before their current hero. They were not interested; they didn't even bother to reply to my letter.

I am forced to add, however, that it is not always backers who promote inaccuracies. Writers, journalists and television interviewers must share a lot of the blame for distorting the truth about many seagoing adventurers. In this respect, the story of Alexander Selkirk is worth mentioning because his famous adventure illustrates some essential lessons which every single-hander should learn: that the solo sailor must decide first whether he intends to operate entirely under his own auspices, or under the patronage of others; that the power of the pen is, and always will be, mightier than the flashing sword of the adventurer. In other words, heroes are created more by words than by their deeds—and deeds were certainly ten-a-penny in those days.

Drake's successful privateering voyage around the world had been repeated with equal success by Thomas Cavendish in the *Desire* (1686–8), and William Dampier in the *St George* (1703–6). In 1709 the privateer *Duke*, captained by Woodes Rogers, called at the island of Más-a-Tierra in the Juan Fernandez group for water and other supplies. Here they found a tattered semi-inarticulate man who, they discovered, had been marooned for four years and four months: none other than Alexander Selkirk, ex-sailing master in the tiny 90 ton *Cinque Ports* under Captain Stradling, who had actually asked to be marooned because he couldn't get on with his notorious captain.

Just as blue-water yachtsmen these days are very aware of each others' trials and tribulations through the inevitable grapevine which exists in every port, and also because of the sparseness of their numbers, so did the pirates intermingle information, ships and people in their own very small world. Rogers had not long before lost sight of *Cinque Ports*, which was still a-privateering, and with whom he had been sailing in company for no better reason than that he had lost contact with his own consort *Fame* just before rounding the Horn. Roger's sailing master on this (as it transpired) sixth circumnavigation was William Dampier, who had captained the fifth ship to sail round the world, and who knew Selkirk to be an excellent and adventurous fellow to have aboard from his experiences with him during an earlier privateering voyage. Nor was this all in a tangled set of coincidences.

In 1680 Bartholomew Sharp, mentioned earlier, was watering his captured Spanish ship off Más-a-Tierra (which he had christened Queen Katharine Island) when three Spanish sail were sighted. Not wanting to get caught with his pants down, Sharp hurriedly recalled his crew from ashore, made sail, and got out of an awkward spot. Unfortunately, in the panic an Indian, known only as Will, was left behind.

Sharp's voyage, since capturing his ship after crossing the Panama Isthmus on foot, had not been particularly successful, so his crew invoked the articles under which nearly all pirates sailed, and he was deposed in favour of one John Watling (after whom Columbus' first island landfall in the New World is still named). Watling proposed a raid on Arica in Chile, which subsequently proved such a disastrous failure that Sharp was voted back as captain. Forty-four dissenters set out in two longboats and returned to the Isthmus (a distance of well over 2000 miles, and a passage preceding Captain Bligh's famous open boat voyage by more than a century), which they re-crossed in getting back to their original fleet in the Caribbean. Sharp and his supporters continued the cruise, this time with some success—although they made one unfortunate mistake when they found 700 pigs of metal on one ship they captured and then sunk, saving just one bar for casting into bullets; only when it was too late did they learn that they had sent to the bottom 699 bars of solid silver. Finally, Sharp sailed south, rounded the Horn, and thus ensured his mark in the long list of maritime 'firsts'.

Among the Isthmus returners, believe it or not, was William Dampier, who certainly was not as cack-handed as some of his compatriots. He remembered Indian Will being marooned, and when he was next in those waters he made a point of calling at Más-a-Tierra to see if the unfortunate man was still there. He was! The date was March 22, 1684.

Now, on January 31, 1709, twenty-five years later, Woodes Rogers, with the indefatigable William Dampier, discovered Alexander Selkirk. When the castaway left with them two weeks later, he had been promoted to captain of a small captured galley, re-named *Increase* by Commander Rogers.

After many adventures in the Pacific, Selkirk eventually arrived back in England in October 1711, to become moderately famous as a result of his lonely ordeal, and (it is said by some) prey to one Daniel Defoe, who stole his remarkable story. It is certainly true that Selkirk met Defoe at the home of a Mrs

Damaris Daniel in Bristol, shortly after his return. It is interesting too to read the following remarks written by William Mavor, a stern critic of Defoe, in 1797.

> ... it should be here remarked what indeed few are ignorant of: that when Selkirk came to England he was advised to put his papers into the hands of the celebrated Daniel Defoe to arrange for publication. But that ingenious literary pirate, converting the original material by the aid of a luxurious fancy into the well-known romance of *Robinson Crusoe*, thus defrauded Selkirk of the emolument which, it was reasonable to suppose, he might have reaped from his unaffected narrative of his solitary occupations and thoughts.

In 1712 Selkirk published *Providence Displayed, or a Surprising Account of one Alexander Selkirk*; in 1719 Daniel Defoe published *Robinson Crusoe*. Whatever the merits of the case, we at least know which book we read now, though I think it is a great shame that the coincidence of combined adventures described briefly here was not included in the splendid fiction of the world famous castaway. Certainly the truth of the matter is much, much stranger than Defoe's fiction—even though the facts would have kept Indian Will and Selkirk forever apart, whereas Crusoe met his Man Friday half way through the book.

Selkirk's share of the prizes taken by Woodes Rogers was £800, so he certainly wasn't poverty stricken as a result of Defoe's piracy. He returned to his native Fifeshire, eloped with a cowherd-ess named Sophia Bruce, but shortly afterwards left her. He spent the rest of his life as a hermit, living for a time in a cave dug in his own garden and always walking the hills alone, speaking to nobody. I think he pined, just as Slocum and so many other singlehanders in later years yearned for the days when they discovered the precise ingredients of solitude which their souls had always needed. That such a discovery is invariably marred by an equal longing for recognition indicates the perverse and still-unsolved complication of the human mind.

So the third important lesson which singlehanders can learn from Selkirk's experiences can be stated thus: Bearing in mind that singlehanded hardly ever means totally self-provided, is the ambition of continuing solitude more persistent than that of personal fame? The answer, regrettably, is nearly always the same: the thrill of achievement—even of survival—demands recognition, and therefore can seldom remain suppressed. To return to the fleshpots is an attempt to attain (again to quote Captain Bartholomew Roberts) 'plenty and satiety, pleasure and ease, liberty and power'.

Although the early sea adventurers were undoubtedly responsible for many original feats, as far as I have been able to discover very few involuntary singlehanded voyages were recorded in those days, and certainly none of them were voluntary.

Richard Falconer, for example, who was born in Somerset about the time Bartholomew Sharp was rounding Cape Horn, went to sea as a cadet in the frigate *Albion* in 1699 and subsequently found himself alone in a small sloop in the Caribbean. Granted leave of absence from his ship, he had joined a logwood trading sloop departing from Port Royal, Jamaica for Campeche on the Panama Isthmus mainland. On a coasting vessel in those waters the ship's boat was frequently towed astern, and Falconer often retired to this secluded place when off watch in order to study. On this occasion a sudden squall, accompanied by heavy rain, snapped the painter—and Falconer found himself adrift, shortly afterwards falling overboard from even this safe refuge in his attempts to attract the attention of his shipmates. He swam for four hours, and then felt his feet touch bottom; incredibly, he had accidentally landed on one of the several low sandbanks, now called Arcas Cays, situated some sixty miles west of Campeche. Here he survived for about a month, making fire by the laborious method of rubbing sticks together, clubbing dim-witted boobies for food, and making a mud reservoir to contain water collected in the frequent rain showers. As a survival exercise, starting with nothing, he did quite well.

But when a small sloop ran aground on his island during a gale in November, Falconer was overjoyed. Four Englishmen were the only crew of this vessel, survivors of a mêlée at Campeche in which (they claimed) Spaniards and Indians had killed four of their number. Realizing that here was his chance to escape from the island, Falconer managed to persuade the four dispirited men that their only hope of survival was to refloat the stranded ship. They toiled for sixteen days to clear a trench in the sand, and laboured so mightily that one of the men died. But on December 31, 1699 they succeeded in their task and the sloop swung to her anchor in deep water, but still close to the beach.

Not unnaturally the four men celebrated their success that same night, drinking more than a fair whack of the rum supplies on board. Falconer passed out, to revive from his stupor next morning only to find that he was alone on board the sloop which had dragged her anchor and drifted out to sea. The sandy islet was nowhere in sight.

This particular drift lasted for thirty days. Falconer seems to have made no attempt to sail the sloop—possibly because the sails had been taken ashore to make a tent during the salvage operation.

At last he drifted close enough to the Isthmus to be rescued by a canoe full of friendly Indians, who salvaged his sloop and took him to the nearest Spanish Governor. Much to his surprise he was treated well, and the Spanish colonists collected money and fitted out another sloop so that he could sail to the rescue of his three mates.

Whether Richard Falconer held the record at that time for the longest singlehanded drift is doubtful, but his story is mentioned because it gives a very good idea of the possibilities which existed for record-breaking voyages in small boats. The pirates and the privateers were here, there and everywhere, and as can be judged from the long and successful haul made by the forty-four led by ex-Captain Watling, no journey by sea (or by land) was impossible if there was treasure at the end of it—or escape from capture.

The Voyages, dangerous Adventures and imminent Escapes of Captain Richard Falconer was published within a few months after *Robinson Crusoe*. But the thrilling events had occurred *twenty years before*. The similarity between the stranding of the sloop and Crusoe's survival through the adequate contents of his ship does not need elaboration. I suspect that Defoe knew as much about Falconer as he did about Selkirk and Indian Will. Why shouldn't he combine them all into one excellent escapist story? Why not indeed? Selkirk had already published his book in 1712; now Falconer and Defoe had published theirs (I wonder *why* they came out so close together?). They all had their chances, but the skilled pen of Daniel Defoe left the work that now remains as a known common denominator.

The backers too are still with us to this day: names are printed on many a company's list of directors whose ancestors controlled ports and otherwise feathered their nests with their four-fifths earnings from the glorious booty of piracy.

British piracy began to decline rapidly from 1721. The reasons are numerous, and mostly unconnected with our subject. But it is interesting to observe that as political pressure began to snap at the heels of the sponsors, so did piracy die. A few freebooters kept going against all odds into the nineteenth and twentieth centuries, but by then they were barely scraping the barrel.

Remembering Captain Bellamy's castigation of the reluctant merchant captain, I cannot help feeling that the spirit of piracy still lingers in the heart of many a modern singlehander. 'Had ye not better make one of us', you can almost hear them repeat, 'than sneak after the arses of those rich villains for employment?' My impression is that sometimes the sponsored are as like-minded in this as those who support themselves, which does not seem to say very much for their loyalty. On the other hand, I don't suppose many pirates or privateers remained particularly loyal to their backers (or the Crown) after they had discovered that 'in the pirate life there is liberty and power'.

The only flaw, which no doubt they all discover in due course, is that the piratical seldom reap more than a brief explosion of publicity from their exploits—which is the sole source of their power—whereas the sponsors invariably go on forever. Drake was the exception—perhaps because he was almost entirely responsible for his own sponsorship.

3
Jaghts, Fore-and-afters and Open Boats

While the British were doing extremely well for themselves in the seventeenth century as pirates, privateers and merchants, industrious Dutch were inventing yachting. The origin of the word is quoted as coming from the Old Dutch *jager*, meaning a hunter or sportsman; the verb was *jagen*, to hunt. So a *jaght-schip* came to mean either a fast vessel, or a ship owned and used by a sportsman. *Jaghts* were at first attached to the Dutch Navy in their capacity as fast ships, and used as naval yachts, revenue cutters and for carrying despatches. Very soon wealthy Dutchmen were launching their own *jaghts* and thoroughly enjoying themselves by imitating famous Dutch naval manoeuvres and battles, for these vessels were fitted out with cannon and all the paraphernalia of war. In addition to the sham fights, reviews and water-parades were held under the command of a *Jaght* Admiral. However, it never seems to have occurred to anybody that they could have some fun racing each other.

With such enthusiasm, it is not surprising that the Dutch were the first to compile data on which they could improve the performance of their *jaghts* (as well as their naval vessels), thus improving on the casual rule-of-thumb designing methods employed elsewhere. Two hundred years were to pass—until about 1850—before the British ceased to follow blindly the Dutch rulings which begat the early fore-and-aft rigged yachts which themselves begat every type of fore-and-aft rigged working vessel in the British Isles: the yachts came first—not the working craft.

My 115 ton deadweight spritsail rigged Thames barge, built in 1897, wore her heavy canvas in much the same manner as many of those Dutch *jaghts* over three centuries ago, although the earliest known illustration showing a sprit-rigged mainsail dates back to 1416. On one or two brief occasions I sailed my barge singlehanded, but the labour involved was considerable. Nevertheless, engineless barges have been traded in this manner, and I believe Captain 'Tubby' Blake achieved an all-time record when he repeatedly sailed his 105 ton *Lancashire* (80′ × 18′) during and just after World War II. Born in 1884, Blake sailed another barge, *Good Templar*, singlehanded from Rotterdam to Maldon in Essex when he was seventy. As these craft set 3000–4000 square feet of working canvas, I doubt if this record will ever be beaten. On the yachting side, J R Elliot sailed his converted spreety *Dipper* mostly alone during several years immediately after the war. She is the largest motorless yacht (73′ × 15′ × 2′6″) to be sailed singlehanded over a protracted period, although of course the cruising grounds were all the time within the Thames Estuary and never more than a dozen miles or so from land.

The Dutch *jaghts* would have been impossible to sail single-handed, even although most of them were smaller than *Dipper*. Heavily sparred, and canvassed with square, as well as fore-and-aft sails—not forgetting their guns and appurtenances—they required large crews.

When the young Charles II was proclaimed King in 1660, he was on a visit to Holland. As he had to return to England quickly, the Prince of Orange loaned him his *jaght* so that he could travel to the Hague in comfort, and from there take ship across the North Sea. This experience so pleased King Charles that he talked of having his own yacht built in England. The Burgomaster of Amsterdam got to hear of this, and immediately promised Charles that in a very short time he would be presented with one. That same year, the first British yacht came to England. Named *Mary* by the delighted King, she measured 52′ × 19′ × 10′; she was fitted with leeboards, carried eight guns and shipped a crew of twenty. Before the spring of 1661 was over two British-built yachts had been launched: *Anne*, for the King's brother, the Duke of York, and *Jenny*, ordered by Charles himself. These were virtually exact copies of *Mary*, though *Ann* drew three feet less water. The Dutch were so pleased that their gift had sparked off such enthusiasm, that they sent over another *jaght*, *Bezan*—a much smaller vessel, measuring only 34' × 14' × 3'6" (similar to Slocum's *Spray*), which the famous diarist Samuel Pepys soon claimed as his own.

By the summer of 1661 there were four yachts in England: two British built and two Dutch. It is not surprising, therefore, that a race was arranged: on October 1 the King wagered £100 that his yacht was faster than his brother's British built vessel. Thus in the space of one year, yachting came to Britain, and Britain invented yacht racing. Incidentally, the Merry Monarch lost the Greenwich to Gravesend morning race, but saved his stake on the return passage. Such was the interest aroused by racing that the very next year, on September 22, 1662, Sir William Petty launched a vessel to his own design of two bottoms, or keels, which he named *Simon and Jude*. Spritsail-rigged, measuring 30' × 10' × 10" and displacing 1·64 tons, she was described as being very seaworthy and extremely fast: she was, in fact, the first catamaran yacht.

It should not be thought that this new sport of yachting was any cheaper then than it is now. The builder of *Ann*, Christopher Pett, quoted £1850 for a replica, excluding guns. So it was not long before the first creditors began to plague the first yachtsmen— and among the creditors were surely some of those large crews.

Yachting as a sport for kings did nothing towards foreshadowing the possibility of one man sailing his own vessel across an ocean. Neither did the varied merchant shipping of the world. But it had been proved that men could survive in small open boats at sea, and certainly whalers and fishermen had been long accustomed to working such craft. The Norwegians had hunted whales off their coast since the ninth century. In the twelfth the Scots established a successful industry in the North Sea off their eastern seaboard. Towards the end of the sixteenth century Basques were whaling in the Bay of Biscay, and later went north to Iceland, Greenland and Newfoundland.

In 1585 the British sent two small exploratory vessels to Greenland: *Sunshine* of 50 tons and twenty-three men, and *Moonshine* of 35 tons and nineteen men; both much smaller than Schouten's *Eendracht*. They returned safely with news of the abundance of seal, walrus and whales in the Davis Straits (named after their commander, Captain John Davis). As though these ships were not small enough, he repeated a second expedition the very next year, again taking these two, plus the 120 ton *Mermaid* as Flagship, and a 13 ton pinnace *North Star* (about as big as a beamy 30 ft yacht) which, not surprisingly, failed to return with the rest.

In 1594 the Dutchman, William Barentz, set off in equally small ships to seek the Northwest Passage to Cathay, failed, tried again, failed, but in 1596 discovered Bear Island and Spitzbergen. When his ship became embayed in ice, he finally landed on Nova Zemlya (already discovered by the English navigator, Willoughby). Here he and his small crew died ashore, his winter quarters and his journal not being discovered until 175 years later, in 1871. However, his consort managed to escape the ice, and they returned to Amsterdam with news of the quantity of whale in the north, ripe for the taking.

So the history of commercial whaling began, and during the next two hundred years the fleets of many countries spread throughout the world, seeking the golden wealth of the rich oil contained in each gigantic carcass. This bloody trade does not concern us here, but the small open boats which actually hunted the whale do.

These double ended whaleboats, clinker-built with planks of not more than half-inch thickness, were generally 25 to 30 ft in length, with a beam of $5-5\frac{1}{2}$ ft, rowing four but more usually five 15 ft oars, with a sixth steering oar. Often these craft lost contact with their mother ship for one reason or another and were forced to make incredibly long voyages. Inevitably the danger, hardships and privation whittled down the crew, who quite often survived only because finally they indulged in cannibalism. The story of the American whaler *Janet* is as representative as any other in this respect, for although the event occurred in 1849 in the Pacific, it could just as easily have taken place in 1749 in the Atlantic, or 1649 in the Arctic, the birthplace of commercial whaling.

Captain Hosmer had left on a three year whaling cruise from Westport, Connecticut in the spring of 1849, and by the end of June he had rounded Cape Horn and was cruising about a thousand miles west of the South American coast at the latitude of Peru. Sperm whales were sighted and three boats were launched, Hosmer taking charge of one of them. Each boat soon made a kill, but by then they were scattered, and since the mother ship could only pick up one crew at a time, and Hosmer's whale was furthest away, he ordered his men to begin to tow the giant carcass towards the *Janet*.

Then the wind freshened, and with the vast bulk of the whale still in tow, somehow the boat capsized. Most of the gear on board was lost, including the compass, a keg of water and the bailer. The crew righted the boat without difficulty, for this was a common enough event, lashed the long oars athwartships to prevent a second capsize, and waited, sitting up to their waists in water, to be rescued. But the *Janet*, although she cruised around the area, failed to spot them, and later that same day she sailed out of their sight.

They managed to survive the gale by sheltering under the lee of their dead whale. Later that first night they saw some ship's lights, which they assumed belonged to *Janet*, and in an attempt to save themselves they hoisted the mast and sail and drove the waterlogged boat towards the lights. But by morning the *Janet* had disappeared. Now they did not even have the shelter of the whale, and without food, water or any navigational instruments, still in a waterlogged boat, their position appeared hopeless.

Somehow, in sheer desperation, they managed to bail out most of the water with their hands. During this laborious effort two of the men fell overboard and were drowned. Two others became delirious and had to be forcibly restrained from jumping overboard. In spite of everything, Captain Hosmer did not give up; he decided to head for Cocos Island, a tiny dot in the vast expanse of ocean roughly a thousand miles away.

Just as for the Polynesians described earlier, the problem of drinking water was solved by occasional showers of rain; food, however, was more difficult. Of the two delirious men, one died after ten days and was pushed overboard. The other? Well, the captain and a man called Cortez were still reasonably fit and it was suggested that one of the three should die so that the other two could live. They drew lots; the sick man lost; he was put to death by opening a vein and the two survivors ate his flesh raw.

Incredibly, after twenty-one days, Captain Hosmer sailed into Chatham Bay, Cocos Island, to find another American whaler, the *Leonidas* of New Bedford, preparing to leave. He had actually made his island landfall over that great distance without any navigational aids whatsoever, and both he and Cortez in due course completely recovered from their ordeal.

Now although this particular small boat voyage occurred in the middle of the nineteenth century, if is not unreasonable to assume that hundreds of similar survival efforts had been made during the

47

previous two hundred or more years. And not only among the whaling fleets, or the pirates, nor, indeed, merchant and naval shipping.

In 1700, Dr James Wallace published in London *An Account of the Islands of Orkney*, containing the following strange report.

> Sometimes about this Country [the Orkneys] are seen these men they call Finn-men. In the year 1682, one was seen in his little Boat at the South end of the Isle of Edz; most of the people of the Isle flock'd to see him, and when they adventur'd to put out a Boat with Men to see if they could apprehend him, he presently fled away most swiftly. And in the year 1684, another was seen from Westra; I must acknowledge it seems a little unaccountable, how these Finn-men should come on this coast, but they must probably be driven by Storms from home, and I cannot tell when they are any way at Sea, how to make their way home again; they have this advantage, that be the Seas never so boisterous their Boat being made of Fish Skins, are so contrived that he can never sink, but is like a Sea-gull swimming on top of the water. His shirt he has is so fastened to the Boat, that no Water can come into his Boat to do him damage, except when he pleases to unty it, which he never does but to ease nature, or when he comes ashore. One of their Boats was catched in Orkney, was sent from thence to Edinburgh, and is to be seen in the Physicians Hall, with the Oar and Dart he makes use of for killing Fish. There is another of their Boats in the Church of Buira in Orkney.

So individual Eskimos arrived from time to time, and were reported in various parts of the British Isles and Europe. Whether they came by design or accident nobody seems to know, but from the way they all seemed deliberately to avoid contact with us 'natives' I think that these 'Finn-men' were actually bent on voyages of exploration—crazy as it may appear to us now. After all, in more recent times the Atlantic has been deliberately crossed and re-crossed in very small folding boats, canoes and dugouts, by men who certainly could never be as skilled and weatherwise as we now know the Eskimos were (and as a few still are).

And it was not only the Eskimos who crossed the Atlantic in small boats. Around 1642, two large dugout canoes arrived in the Azores loaded with two families of red men with their goods and chattels, who obviously were intent on finding new pastures. Again, in his book *Lonely Voyagers* Jean Merrien quotes another 'red and strange' man who arrived on the coast of Spain at about this period, alone this time but once again in 'a hollowed tree' or dugout canoe. Unfortunately, on this occasion the religious zeal of the Spaniards was apparently of more importance to them than discovering some simple facts about the red man's voyage and origin. He survived the Atlantic crossing only to succumb to their ministrations.

There are other examples, too, of even earlier voyages from west to east, but although there is no doubt that men actually crossed the Atlantic individually and in convoy in an easterly direction on many occasions, virtually no useful contact seemed to have been made with them at the time—or if the poor devils were captured, 'converting the heathen' was generally regarded as being of greater importance than otherwise attempting to communicate with them. It is impossible to say whether the following account is about a singlehanded ocean voyager who lost his boat, but the details indicate the sort of treatment imposed on anybody who was not a Christian.

At the time of King Henry II, when Bartholomew de Glanville was custodian at Orford Castle, it happened that some fishermen there, whilst fishing in the sea, caught a merman in their nets. He was taken to the aforesaid castellan for him to see. He was completely naked, and in all his members were like human form, but he was heavily covered with hair which was ragged and shaggy in appearance, his beard was long and pointed, and his chest very hairy and shaggy. The aforesaid Knight had him held in custody for a long time, day and night, so that he could not return to the sea. He ate fish, raw or cooked, but squeezed the raw fish vigorously between his hands, until the juice ran out, and then ate them. Furthermore, he would not, or rather could not, utter a word, although suspended by his feet, and most harshly tortured. When taken to church, he showed no sign of reverence, nor any inclination to believe anything sacred. He always went to rest immediately at sunset, remaining till sunrise. On one occasion he was taken to the seashore and allowed to go in to the sea, but strong nets, in three lines were set up before him. Soon, plunging into the deep sea, he repeatedly went through the nets, and emerged from the depths; and he watched the spectators on the shore for a long time, frequently immersing himself, and after a little, re-emerging as if mocking the spectators because he had evaded their nets. When he had played in the sea in this fashion for a long time, and all hope of his returning had been lost, he came back to them of his own free will, swimming in the waves. He thus remained with them for two more months, but shortly afterwards he was negligently guarded, and being looked on with revulsion, he fled in secret to the sea, and was not seen again. Whether this was a mortal man, whether a fish in human form, or whether an evil spirit in a human form, such as was read of in the life of the blessed Audoenus, cannot be determined easily, mainly because so many marvels have been told, by so many people, about these events.

Orford Castle, situated on the nose of the head which mapmakers call East Anglia, was completed in 1165; Henry II died in 1189. So this very strange capture occurred within the twenty-four years between. There are other accounts of mermen, but this is the best authenticated and probably the most accurate. These strange men had to come from somewhere, and one possible explanation is that they, like the Eskimos* and the 'red men', came from across the Atlantic.

I have often wondered whether Lieutenant William Bligh of the *Bounty* would have attempted his 3618 mile open boat voyage after the mutiny, instead of holeing up on the nearest island, if he had not known something about these and other voyages. The launch in which he and eighteen loyal crew rowed and sailed was 23 ft long, and when loaded with the water, provisions and sundry equipment which Fletcher Christian allowed them to take, the

---

*Roger Pilkington in *Small Boat to Northern Germany* (Macmillan, 1970) writes that there is a kayak in the Schiffergesellchaft at Lubeck. It was found drifting in the Skaggerrak in 1607. The Eskimo was upright in his seat, reduced to a skeleton inside his skin. The kayak was salvaged with the man *in situ*, and they were exhibited like this for many years. I am indebted to Philip Banbury for this information, who also drew my attention to *The Story of Our Kayak and Some Others*, a presidential address to the Aberdeen Medico-Chirurgical Society by William Clark Souter on October 26, 1933, which recounts stories and lists facts about many kayaks which were discovered around the British Isles from before 1365, ranging in length from 11'8½" to 24'4", and in beam from 1'4½" to 2'3". There seems little doubt that the first singlehanded transatlantic voyages were accomplished by Eskimos.

freeboard was said to have been reduced to seven inches. What was the safety margin of Captain Watling's longboats, loaded with forty-four fully armed pirates, coasting along a Spanish-held shore which was as hostile to them as the natives on the islands among which Bligh was forced to find his way? I suspect that Bligh knew far more about open boat voyaging than we credit him; all the accounts which I have read tend to glorify this voyage of 1789 as a first-ever, whereas I hope I have shown that it was merely one of many—albeit an outstandingly seamanlike accomplishment.

Ten years later, in 1799, there occurred the first semi-voluntary voyage in a small open boat, which in my opinion was even more remarkable than either Watling's or Bligh's efforts. Semi-voluntary because the six men involved did not *have* to make the attempt: that they were deserters from the British Army garrison on the island of St Helena in the South Atlantic does not exactly put them in the same category as yachtsmen, but certainly they had some free will in the matter and could have refused.

On December 12, 1799 a Court of Inquiry was held at St Helena before Captain Desfontain, President, Lieutenant B Hudson and Ensign Young. The following statement was made by John Brown, one of the survivors of the voyage, under oath. I think it is worth quoting in full.

In June 1799 I belonged to the first company of artillery, in this garrison, and on the 10th of that month, about half an hour before parade time, McKinnon, gunner and orderly of the second company, asked me if I was willing to go with him on board of an American ship, called the *Columbia*, Captain Henry Lelar, the only ship then in the roads. After some conversation I agreed and met him about seven o'clock, at the playhouse, where I found one McQuin, of Major Seale's company, another man called Brighouse, another named Parr, and the sixth, Matthew Conway.

Parr was a good seaman, and said he would take us to the island of Ascension, or lie off the harbour till the *Columbia* could weigh anchor and come out. We went down about eight o'clock to the West Rock, where the American boat, manned with three seamen, was waiting for us and took us alongside the *Columbia*. We went on board; Parr went down into the cabin, and we changed our clothes, after having been on board half an hour.

Brighouse and Conway proposed to cut a whaleboat out of the harbour, to prevent the *Columbia* from being suspected. This they accomplished, taking in her a coil of rope, five oars, and a large stone by which she was moored.

We observed lanterns passing on the line towards the Sea Gate, and hearing a noise, thought we were missed and sought for. We immediately embarked in the whaleboat, with about twenty-five pounds of bread in a bag, and a small keg of water, supposed to contain three gallons, and one quadrant, given to us by the commanding officer of the *Columbia*.

We then left the ship, pulling with two oars only, to get ahead of her. The boat was half full of water, and we had nothing to bail it out. In this condition we rode out to sea, and lay off the island at a great distance, in hourly expectation of the American ship taking us up.

About twelve o'clock the second day, no ship appearing, by Parr's advice we bore away, steering N by W, and then NNW for the island of Ascension, using our handkerchiefs as substitutes for sails. We met with a gale of wind, which continued two days; the weather then became very fine, and we supposed we had run about ten miles an hour. McKinnon kept a reckoning with pen, ink, and paper, with which, together with maps and charts, we were supplied by the *Columbia*.

We continued our course till about the 18th in the morning, when we saw a number of birds, but no land. About twelve that day, Parr said he was sure we must be past the island, accounting it to be 800 miles from St Helena. Each of us then took off our shirts, and with them we made a small spritsail, lacing our jackets and trousers at the waistband to keep us warm; and then altering our course to W by N, thinking to make Rio de Janerio, on the American coast. Provisions running very short, we allowed ourselves only one ounce of bread, and two mouthfulls of water for twenty-four hours.

On the 25th all our provisions were expended. On the 27th McQuin put a piece of bamboo in his mouth to chew, and we all followed his example. On that night of that day it was my turn to steer the boat, and recollecting to have read of persons in our situation eating their shoes, I cut a piece off one of mine; but being soaked with salt water, I was obliged to spit it out, and take the inside sole, of which I ate a part, and distributed the remainder to the rest; but we found no benefit from it.

On the first of July Parr caught a dolphin, with a gaff that had been left in the boat. We all fell on our knees, and thanked God for his goodness to us. We tore up the fish, and hung it to dry; about four we ate part of it, which agreed with us pretty well. On this fish we subsisted till the 4th; about eleven o'clock, when finding the whole consumed, Parr, Brighouse, Conway and myself proposed to scuttle the boat, and let her go down, to put us out of our misery; the other two objected, observing that God, who had made man, always found him something to eat.

On the 5th, about eleven, McKinnon proposed that it would be better to cast lots for one of us to die, in order to save the rest, to which we consented. William Parr, being seized two days before with the spotted fever, was excluded. He wrote the numbers and put them into a hat. We drew them out blindfolded, and put them in our pockets. Parr then asked whose lot it was to die; none of us knowing what number we had in our pocket, it was agreed that number five should die, and the lots being unfolded, McKinnon's was the fatal number.

We had concluded that he on whom the lot fell should bleed himself to death, for which purpose we had provided ourselves with sharpened nails, which we got from the boat. With one of these McKinnon cut himself in three places; in his foot, hand, and wrist; and praying to God to forgive his sins, he died in about a quarter of an hour.

Before he was quite cold, Brighouse, with one of the nails, cut a piece of flesh off his thigh and hung it up, leaving his body in the boat. About three hours afterwards we all ate of it, but only in very small quantity. We dipped the body every two hours on the sea to preserve it. Parr having found a piece of slate in the bottom of the boat, he sharpened it on the large stone, and with it cut another piece off the thigh, which lasted us till the 8th; when it being my watch, and observing the water, about break of day, to change colour, I called the rest, thinking that we were near the shore, but saw no land, it not being quite daylight.

As soon as day appeared, we discovered land right ahead, and steered towards it. About eight in the morning we were close to the shore. There being a heavy surf, we endeavoured to turn the boat's head to it, but being very weak, we were unable. Soon afterwards the boat upset. Parr, Conway, and myself got on shore, but McQuin and Brighouse were drowned.

We discovered a small hut on the beach, in which were an Indian and his mother, who spoke Portuguese; and I understanding that language, learned that there was a village, about three miles distant, called Belmont. The Indian went to the village, with the information that the French had landed; and in about two hours the governor of the village, a clergyman, and several armed men, took Conway and Parr, tied them by their hands and feet, and slinging them on a bamboo stick, conveyed them to the village. I being very weak, remained in the hut some time, but was afterwards taken.

On our telling them we were English, we were immediately released, and three hammocks provided, in which we were taken to the governor's house, who resigned to us his own bed, and gave us milk and rice to eat; but as we had taken no food for a considerable time, we were jaw-locked, and continued so till the 23rd. During this time our host wrote to the governor of St Salvador, who sent a schooner to Porto Seguro to take us to St Salvador. We were conducted on horseback to Porto Seguro, passing through Santa Crux, where we remained about ten days. We afterwards embarked; and on our arrival at St Salvador, Parr, on being questioned by the governor, told him that our ship had foundered at sea, and that we had saved ourselves in the boat; that the ship's name was the *Sally* of Liverpool, that she belonged to his father, and was last from Cape Corse Castle, on the coast of Africa, to touch at Ascension for turtle, and then bound for Jamaica. Parr likewise said that he was the captain.

We remained at St Salvador about thirteen days, during which time the inhabitants made up a subscription of £200 each man. We then embarked in the *Maria*, a Portuguese ship, for Lisbon; Parr as mate, Conway as boatswain's mate, and myself, being sickly, as a passenger. In thirteen days we arrived at Rio de Janerio. Parr and Conway sailed for Lisbon, and I was left in the hospital.

In about three months, Captain Elphinstone, of the *Diamond*, pressed me into His Majesty's service, giving me the choice of remaining in that station, or to proceed to the Admiral at the Cape. I preferred the latter, and was put, with seven suspected deserters, on board the *Ann*, a Botany Bay ship, in irons, with the convicts. When I arrived at the Cape, I was put on board the *Lancaster*, of sixty-four guns. I never entered, but at length received my discharge; since which I engaged in the *Duke of Clarence* as a seaman. I was determined to surrender myself the first opportunity, in order to relate my sufferings to the men of this garrison, and to deter others from attempting so mad a scheme.

This voyage of rather more than 2500 miles in twenty-eight days remains the fastest long distance rowing record to this day, and the first Atlantic crossing (or perhaps more accurately, part-crossing) by a boat propelled only by oars. That they frequently used their clothing as makeshift sails, and were no doubt helped considerably by the southeast Trade Winds, is not entirely relevant: they left St Helena with five oars and no sails, and averaged nearly 90 miles per day; just under a century later, Harbo and Samuelson rowed from New York to the Isles of Scilly, equipped with five pairs of oars, and averaged 56 m.p.d. They, too, probably helped their 18 ft 4 in double-ender *Richard K Fox* along with 'sails' of some kind whenever the wind was fair. The fastest *singlehanded* Atlantic rowing crossing was made by Sidney Genders (British) in 1970, when he averaged 37 m.p.d. rowing his 19 ft 9 in *Khaggavisana* from Sennen Cove, Land's End, via the Canary Islands and Antigua to Miami, Florida. On such a route, he too could have 'sailed' on many occasions, using the northeast Trades.

I have had to leave out a great deal of information which is not entirely relevant to the main subject of singlehanded voyages, dealing with the growth of the sport of yachting in various countries, and placing early and recent passages in a broader context. For example, the 98 ton American sloop *Union*, which had sailed from Newport, Rhode Island (one of the famous whaling harbours) on August 1, 1794, returned just under two years later on July 8, 1796 having circumnavigated westabout, thus becoming the very first fore-and-aft rigged vessel to double Cape Horn and to sail round the world—with the very creditable sea-time average sailing speed of 130 m.p.d. That the twenty-two men who comprised her crew were commanded by nineteen year old John Boit, Jr (he was just twenty-one when he brought his ship back to Rhode Island) makes this little known 'first' all the more remarkable.

Another almost unknown voyage which began in 1793 and finished eleven years later as the first circumnavigation by Japanese seamen, was the Marco Polo-like journey of four sailors from Mitsu: Tsudayuu, Sahei, Gihei and Tajuu. In November 1793 they rowed with twelve shipmates from Ishimaki towards Edo-Omote to trade a cargo of rice. During the passage a bad storm drove them off course and out into the vast Pacific. They were adrift for over six months.

November 27, 1793	Departed from Ishimaki.
November 29, 1793	Driven off course by storm.
June 4, 1794	Landed at Tangeratsukestro in Russia; stayed ten months.
April 3, 1795	Sailed to Ohootsukai.
August 18, 1795	Travelled to Yakoutsuka.
November 24, 1795	Crossed Siberia.
January 24, 1796	Arrived Erikoutsuka; worked here for seven years.
April 27, 1803	Travelled to Bizerivolka.
May 16, 1803	Granted audience with Czarina; given permission to return to Japan.
June 1803	Departed Kanashina; landed in Britain, Crossed Atlantic to South America, and thence via Cape Horn to Hawaii.
July 1804	Arrived Kamuchakka.
September 1804	Arrived Nagasaki.

There were sixteen men at the start, and ten arrived to have audience with the Czarina. Only the four named chose to leave Russia and return to their homeland. In many respects, this prolonged journey is possibly the most remarkable of all the 'firsts' among the early circumnavigators.

The pioneering work has been completed. We have followed the adventures of but a few of the very many who must have criss-crossed the oceans of the world in every conceivable type of small craft—canoes, rafts and probably anything else which floated. Now, approximately 1300 years after Brendan crossed the Atlantic, we leave the involuntary small boat voyages to investigate the phenomenon of those who intentionally set forth alone to cross an ocean or to sail round the world.

4
The First Solo~
cruising Yachtsmen

Although I have shown that many small boat voyages had been accomplished since Brendan, some of them singlehanded, it is impossible to state with any certainty who was actually the first person to cross an ocean, or indeed any stretch of water, entirely voluntarily, unsponsored and without thought of reward—in other words, to name the first solo-cruising true yachtsman.

One of the earliest to apply for a passport for such an attempt was a Dutch surgeon, Henry de Voogt. In 1601, addressing the Prince of Aremberg, he requested a permit to travel 'in a little rowing boat . . . quite alone, and with the aid of none but our Lord God Almighty' from Flushing to London. That his passport was approved on April 19, 1601 does not, unfortunately, prove that he actually set forth.

Equally, there is no evidence to prove that in 1800 a Captain Cleveland of Salem, Massachusetts actually made a singlehanded voyage from Cape Town across the Indian and Pacific oceans to Alaska in a 15 ft open boat. It seems unlikely that such a trip could be made without public recognition. (These possible 'firsts' were quoted by Jean Merrien in *Lonely Voyagers*.)

Nor is very much known of the American, J M Crenston, who in 1849 was supposed to have sailed his 40 ft cutter *Tocca* from New Bedford, via either Cape Horn or the Magellan Straits, to San Francisco—a distance of 13,000 miles in 226 days. Was he one of the forty-niners? Did he have a crew? Or was he the skipper of a small trading vessel who decided that the extremely high rates of passage money paid out by gold-rush enthusiasts of that hectic period would more than compensate him for all the desperate effort involved in getting them to the nearest port to Sacramento Valley and the even more fabulous Sutter's Creek? In those days vessels were generally measured by their length of straight keel, and a 40 footer could easily mean a length of hull of 50 ft or more. A cutter of 40 ft keel length could carry a dozen or more people in a rough comfort which today we would find intolerable; if the prospective miners also helped as crew, further space would be saved. I suspect that the skipper himself also lusted after gold, since it must have been apparent to him that once he arrived at San Francisco he would never find a crew for the return voyage. Dozens of square-rigged ships suffered in the same way while gold fever was rife during the years 1848–51. Thus I very much doubt that *Tocca*'s voyage was singlehanded.

But in 1851 there occurred an event which I am sure was more effectively responsible for the introduction of voluntary trans-ocean voyaging than anything I have described so far. This was the first crossing of the Atlantic by a racing yacht for the specific purpose of sport—none other than the famous schooner *America*. Nearly everybody knows something of her famous Cup, although few seem to have connected her twenty-day New York to Le Havre voyage with the subsequent outbreak of small boat trans-atlantic crossings. *America*'s Cup still belongs to America, but the idea of crossing an ocean purely for the sport of it, which now has worldwide acceptance, could only have originated from this rakish racer (146 tons displacement, 101'9" × 23' × 11') which beat such merry hell out of all her British opponents. Queen Victoria most definitely was *not* amused, nor were the patriotic British public; the Squadron were shocked from truck to keelson by her many, apparently effortless, wins.

When *America* was finally sailed back to the States, in 1860, having passed through the hands of four British owners, she left behind her fierce arguments concerning the pros and cons of her design, sails, and the handling by her original American crew, all of which were the cause of much rethinking by British yacht designers. Between 1852 and 1865 there developed a craze for centreboarders, which was followed by a yawl rig craze, and finally total elimination of the Dutch 'cod's head and mackerel's tail' theory, which had already been seriously challenged by the hollow bowed, cutter rigged, British *Mosquito* as early as 1848, although Squadron-type blind prejudice had failed to accept the obvious truth that the design was an improvement.

59

On June 22, 1857 the 43 ft ketch *Charter Oak* sailed from New York towards Liverpool. Captain C R Webb and two crew set out for some reason which remains obscure, but as one of the crew was washed overboard on the very first night at sea, and the ship was recorded as arriving in Liverpool on July 27, we have this evidence of the first two-man (albeit involuntary) transatlantic crossing. I expect that in due course somebody will discover facts of an even earlier voyage, but I will be a little surprised if it happened before *America* awoke the world of yachtsmen to deep-water cruising and passage making possibilities.

After *Charter Oak* there was (as far as I can discover) a pause of nine years while the American Civil War brewed, simmered, and finally boiled over. I cannot even begin to go into the complexities of American politics immediately after the Civil War ended in 1865; suffice it to say that this was the period of 'carpetbaggers', scallywags, tricksters, shysters—of just about anything immoral. If a man could swindle the public without getting in jail he was 'smart'. Most Americans actually admired such trickiness, providing they were not the ones who had been caught out. This was the beginning of the great American method of 'hustling' business.

Thus I am not surprised that the very next two-man crossing of the Atlantic was also the first boating publicity stunt. Painted on the galvanized iron sides of the double-ender *Red, White and Blue* were the words INGERSOLL'S IMPROVED METALLIC LIFE BOAT. Skippered by Americans William Hudson and Frank E Fitch (and a pet dog), this vessel left New York on July 9, 1866 and arrived at Deal in Kent, well up the English Channel, on August 15. Note that although she was small ($26' \times 6'1''$), she was ship-rigged: i.e. three-masted, and square-rigged on all of them; she even carried tiny stuns'ls!

She was the first of very many similar stunts which followed.

During the same year, departing from Boston on July 11 and arriving at Cowes, Isle of Wight on July 30 having sailed about 2900 miles in nineteen days, nineteen hours and twenty minutes, the 48 ft sloop *Alice*, owned by American T C Appleton, with Captain Clarn and an all-American crew of three seamen and a cook, plus two passengers (one of whom was the poet Longfellow's son) was probably the first smallish yacht to cross the Atlantic since the *America*. She took slightly less time.

Next came the first small boat to complete an ocean crossing without her crew. The ketch *John T Ford* ($22'6'' \times 7'$) was launched at Baltimore specifically for displaying at the First Paris Boat Exhibition of 1867 after sailing across the Atlantic. She sailed from her home port on June 22 with a crew of four: Gould (skipper), Shering, Armstrong and Murphy (boy). They put into Halifax, sailing from there on July 16. On August 19, when they were quite close to the south coast of Ireland and running before a gale towards Cork, she capsized. The skipper, mate and boy were drowned, but Armstrong hung on to the wreck for $87\frac{1}{2}$ hours, until he was rescued by the ship *Aerolite* of Liverpool. *John T Ford* finally drifted ashore at Tacumshane on the Wexford coast on September 6, thereby completing the transatlantic passage unmanned.

Next came the trimaran-raft *Nonpareil*—a suitable name if ever there was one. Again, this voyage was a publicity stunt, to advertize the unsinkability of this 'perfect life-saver'. Three $25' \times 2'6''$ inflatable rubber cylinders supported a wooden platform $20' \times 11'6''$ on which was erected a *tent* (that must have shaken all true-blue yachtsmen when they saw it). She was schooner rigged, the masts being stepped on the platform. Four dagger boards could be inserted between the cylinders to give some lateral resistance to drift and assist steering. The crew consisted of an American skipper John Mikes and two Prussians, George Miller and Jerry Mallene (who were said to be unable to speak English; I therefore conclude that these names have been anglicized). *Nonpareil* sailed from New York on June 4, 1868, survived some very bad weather during which she hove-to on seven occasions, and arrived at Southampton on July 25. Although she is generally described as a raft, in my opinion since she could be hove-to she was obviously always under control: therefore I regard this voyage as the first trimaran crossing of the Atlantic, and *not* the first raft crossing.

All the voyages so far have been from west to east—the easy way, helped by the Gulf Stream and the prevailing westerly winds—with the sole exception (of those mentioned) of *America*'s return to the States in 1860. The next Atlantic crossing was from east to west, made by the tiny 20 ft *City of Ragusa* in 1870. Between this and *Nonpareil*'s voyage, however, we must divert our attention to the first genuine singlehanded long distance voyage which was both entirely voluntary and completely successful.

The instigators of British long distance singlehanded yacht cruising are generally quoted as being John MacGregor and

R T McMullen. In my opinion, neither qualify. It is true that John MacGregor made a singlehanded voyage from London to the First Paris Boat Exhibition and back in his 21 ft yawl *Rob Roy* in 1867, and that his book *The Voyage Alone in the Yawl Rob Roy* created a good deal of interest when it was published in that same year. But a cross-Channel cruise is hardly a basis for eulogy in the context of our subject.

Although much has been written about Richard Turrel McMullen since he published his famous book *Down Channel* in 1869, it is not generally stated that he did not voluntarily attempt to cruise singlehanded until 1873, when he sailed *Procyon* from Greenhithe to the Isle of Wight, although he had learned to sail in the 20 ft cutter *Leo* as long ago as 1850 when he was twenty. *Procyon*, a lug yawl ($28'6'' \times 7'$), was fitted with a centreplate. In 1877 McMullen sailed his much larger gaff yawl *Orion* ($48'3'' \times 10'2'' \times 7'$) singlehanded from Cherbourg to the London River, but this was brought about by his dismissing two slovenly deckhands in the French port. For some unaccountable reason a great deal of fuss has since been made in yachting circles about this voyage in the 'heavily sparred' *Orion*. In fact she was originally only 42 ft overall and 38 ft between perpendiculars. Lengthened 6 ft 3 in by the stern in 1873, the original $16\frac{1}{2}$ net registered tons was thereby increased to $19\frac{1}{2}$ tons. At the same time, her rig was altered from cutter to yawl—much easier for a singlehander to handle. Now, when she was rigged as a cutter *Orion*'s boom was 35 ft, gaff 25 ft, with a hoist of 25 ft. Slocum's *Spray*, before conversion to a yawl, carried a 34 ft boom and 19 ft gaff, with a hoist of $28\frac{1}{2}$ ft. When *Orion* was sailed cross-Channel single-handed as a yawl, her rig (particularly the boom) was considerably reduced from the above cutter measurements; Slocum sailed *Spray* from Nova Scotia to Gibraltar, and then re-crossed the Atlantic to Brazil, all in 1895, before he cut down his rig to more manageable proportions. Yet I have never seen anything in print about the 'heavily sparred *Spray*'. So here is another example of a persisting myth like that of Drake discovering the Horn.

Before leaving McMullen, a short quotation from *Down Channel* will be of interest since it defines a British yachtsman's opinion of the American stunt voyages I have mentioned so far.

> In my turn I was cut out by the Metallic Lifeboat Company of New York, who, a few years ago, found men willing, in advertising their patent, to risk starvation by crossing the

Atlantic, and exhibiting the *Red, White and Blue* at the Crystal Palace.

I have never sailed in one of these lifeboats, which, according to all accounts, possess the rare advantage of being able to turn over in a heavy sea without foundering, and for a change, give the crew a ride on the bottom, until by accident or design they come right side up again, and allow the men to get inside and have something to eat.

The singlehanded potterings of MacGregor and McMullen were surpassed by the undoubted eccentricity of Empson Edward Middleton who in 1869 was the first man to plan and execute, entirely on his own and unsponsored, a major singlehanded voyage. In the gaff yawl *Kate* (23′ × 7′ × 2′9″) he circumnavigated England in a clockwise direction from London to London, via the Crinan Canal from Greenock to Grangemouth in Scotland, in 101 days, including voluntary service in the Southwold lifeboat to the rescue of a coasting sailing ship during a twelve day wait in that harbour for the exceptional equinoctial gales to abate.

Compared with *Orion* and *Spray*, *Kate*'s sail plan seems tiny—boom 11½ ft, hoist 13 ft, gaff 10 ft—but she had a 675 lbs iron keel, a 450 lbs iron keelson, and carried 1230 lbs of internal ballast; the only auxiliary was a pair of sweeps, which Middleton called paddles, and at which he toiled frequently for many consecutive hours in order to save his tide around some headland, or to make some of his fifty-nine ports of call in a flat calm.

Middleton was the type of eccentric whose self-discipline was probably in the same class as Brendan's. The only reward he sought was recognition of his many eccentricities. He had a private income, so money did not play a particularly important part in his life (although he kept a meticulous account of his expenditure), but he also had a whole host of ideas which he wished to bring to fruition: from his complex translation of Virgil (which was a flop), to castigating the Yacht Racing Association on their current system of measurement, to flat earth theories, to inventing floating harbours (an astonishing preview of the Mulberry Harbours used in the invasion of Normandy in World War II, and what are now known as yacht marinas), to an overwhelming ambition to publish in large quantities his favourite book, Aristotle's *Ethics*, 'in large print, for the poor to read'.

Whatever his faults, however, Middleton proved by example

exactly what could be accomplished in a small boat, and if his main diet throughout the voyage of sherry and raw eggs was considered of doubtful advantage even in those eccentric days, when *The Cruise of the Kate* was published in 1870 nobody could deny that he was the first man to sail alone around England, and that his exploit 'was to be admired for its audacity'.

From 1869 we turn again to transatlantic voyages, and the first east to west crossing, in 1870. *City of Ragusa* (20′ × 6′ × 2′2″) had been a lifeboat on the ship *Breeze*, which had foundered in the Irish Sea; she had carried fourteen survivors to the Isle of Man. There she was purchased by an American, John C Buckley, who converted her and rigged her as a yawl. Buckley must have been as eccentric as Middleton, for the *Illustrated London News* of June 25, 1870 printed an artist's impression of the boat which shows a large, six-bladed windmill attached to the mizzen, which apparently was intended to drive a two-bladed propeller through gearing and thus enable the vessel to proceed westwards 'into the eye of the wind, without having to tack'. In fact, it was never used, though the principle has since been demonstrated to work.

With an Austrian, Nicholas Primoraz, and a small dog as crew, Buckley sailed from Liverpool on June 3, 1870. They landed at Cork on June 11, and left on the 17th. By August 6 they were only about 40 miles off the Newfoundland coast, and on the 9th, just south of Cape Race, they stretched their legs on board the ship *Maxwell*, bound from Greenock to Quebec. The unfortunate dog died on August 28 (why *do* people have to subject animals to such appalling conditions?) and they survived 'a fearful gale' on September 4. On September 9, 1870 they landed at Boston, Massachusetts having sailed 2584 miles from Cork in eighty-four days, averaging 30·7 m.p.d.

Since the American Civil War, then, variously crewed small boats had crossed the Atlantic in 1866, 1867, 1868 and 1870, and E E Middleton had circumnavigated Britain singlehanded in 1869. All of these craft inevitably contributed a 'first' of one sort or another. However, yachtsmanlike, R T McMullen continued to disapprove.

> My opinion has often been asked about these lifeboats crossing the Atlantic [he wrote in *Down Channel*]. The one referred to [*Red, White and Blue*] had an advertisement of the builders on the bow, and was, one may reasonably suppose, either lent or given to the adventurers to make

what they could out of it—by exhibition. After her return from the Paris Exhibition she lay astern of the *Orion* in Greenhithe Creek, until she was taken back to America on a ship's deck. I have always understood that, financially, she was a failure, chiefly owing to her being exhibited as a full-rigged ship, with royals and studdingsails set, which was manifestly too preposterous even for the credulity of the shallowest landlubber. Others have crossed in emulation of that feat,, but all apparently with a view to make dollars by exhibition, which is so repugnant to British taste that they have left our shores no better freighted than they came. That the boat will not sink is great ground of confidence; but, after the first success, they who adventure on a similar voyage expose themselves to hardships, and the chance of terrible privations, for no useful purpose. I intend no disparagement to American enterprise when I state my belief that thousands from our side would be willing to perform the same feat provided they had a better object in view than any we have as yet seen.

Prejudiced, stiff-upper-lip conservatism or not, McMullen had a point. Apart from *City of Ragusa* (and of course such genuine yachts as *America* and *Alice*), the transatlantic voyages *had* been directed towards the profit motive. It is more than likely that Buckley's voyage was also intended as publicity for his sailing-into-the-eye-of-the-wind device, otherwise what prompted this American to cross the hard way, from east to west?

The point must be made here that many other transatlantic sailing records were being created around this period, and it must not be assumed that only the few very small boats which I have named were crossing the Atlantic at this time. For example, in December, 1866 three large yacht schooners, *Henrietta*, *Fleetwing* and *Vesta*, each exceeding 200 tons displacement and therefore much larger than the 146 ton, 101 ft *America*, raced from Sandy Hook to the Isle of Wight in thirteen days, twenty-two hours; fourteen days, six hours, ten minutes; and fourteen days, six hours, fifty minutes respectively; their best twenty-four hour runs were 280, 260 and 277 miles respectively. In 1868 the schooner rigged yacht *Sappho* crossed from Sandy Hook to Falmouth in fourteen days, and in 1869 she raced from Sandy Hook to Queenstown in twelve days, nine hours, thirty minutes, her best day's run being 316 miles. In the reverse direction, although she was not a yacht, I think it is worth mentioning the extraordinary unbeaten record of the American packet ship *Emerald*, Captain Phillip Fox. This loftily rigged clipper, crossing skysail yards, was small by comparison with some of the later yachts—only 110' × 27' and 359 tons deadweight—yet in 1824 she dropped her moorings in the River Mersey at 1500 hours on February 20, and hove-to for a pilot off Boston Light at 1500 on March 8: Liverpool to Boston in exactly seventeen days! Several other square-riggers beat this time—the fastest being the 1679 ton clipper *Andrew Jackson*: Liverpool to New York in a fraction under fifteen days during 1860—but except for one ship they were all much larger vessels, generally exceeding *Emerald*'s tonnage by two to as much as five times. The one exception was *Josephine* of only 148 tons; she crossed from Belfast, Ireland to New York in just over sixteen days during March and April of 1830. There was also the packet ship *Columbia*, 492 tons, which crossed from Portsmouth to New York in fifteen days, twenty-three hours in April 1830.

So the Atlantic Ocean was a very busy place during the early years of small boat crossings, which was just as well because McMullen's polite tirade against the stunters would have been much more valid if they had not all been able to speak many ships en route in order to obtain positions, renew their food and water supplies, and sometimes go aboard for a meal or to stretch their cramped limbs. *City of Ragusa*, for example, spoke ten ships, and her crew actually boarded two of them.

The east to west passage of the 'windmill yacht' in 1870 seems to have been the end of further small boat crossings for a period of six years. So far, all of them had been American inspired, and I suspect that this gap can be traced to the appalling uncertainties which continued to rend that country after the Civil War. President Johnson was impeached in 1868, and there followed a chaos of graft, speculation, depression and bankruptcies, today castigated as 'the ugly face of capitalism'. There appears to be no other reason why dollar-earning by exhibition (in McMullen's opinion) should have been suspended for six years, although I cannot be absolutely certain that some hitherto unreported attempts were not made during this period.

So until the year 1876, as far as I am aware, only the Englishman E E Middleton had ventured on an unsponsored, singlehanded voyage of any worthwhile length.

On July 4, 1776 the American Declaration of Independence had been approved (although it was not signed until August 2). One hundred years later a twenty-nine year old Danish-born, naturalized American, Grand Banks fisherman Alfred Johnson decided to celebrate the historic event by sailing a 20 ft dory across the Atlantic, and then shipping it back to America in time for the Great Philadelphia Exhibition of that centenary year. He named his dory *Centennial.* So again, we find the profit motive!

Or do we? By all accounts Johnson was a modest man, and perhaps I do him an injustice by emphasizing his original plan—which undoubtedly would have removed his amateur status. As it happened, the voyage took much longer than anticipated, and he was far too late to get to the Exhibition. So in my opinion Johnson remained an amateur, and as such he may be described as the first-ever voluntary, unsponsored, transatlantic singlehander: and although he was a professional fisherman, I can see no reason why he should not be classified as a yachtsman in reference to this voyage. He did it, he said, to prove that nothing was impossible to an American seaman. This reason cannot properly be classified as either sport or pleasure, but it seems to be no more unreasonable than Mallory's excuse for climbing Everest: 'Because it's there.' The magazine *Forest and Stream* summed up the negative aspect rather neatly when the editor sarcastically philosophized: 'If Mr Johnson safely crosses the Atlantic it is not probable that his crossing will materially affect the travel by steamer.' It didn't. But this first transocean singlehander certainly affected future travel by small boats. So at last a fresh page in the record book could be opened and a new title printed across the top: TRANSOCEAN SINGLEHANDERS.

Johnson's dory was decked all over, apart from a small cockpit fitted with a canvas apron which he could lace around his body. The boat (20' × 5'10") was rigged as a gaff cutter with a short bowsprit and she crossed one squaresail yard. Some internal ballast was carried, and she had a loaded freeboard of 12 in. He sailed from Gloucester on June 15, 1876, put into Shag Harbour, Nova Scotia a week later, and finally took his departure towards Liverpool on June 25. Shortly afterwards he ran into his first gale, and lost some of his provisions when a big sea broke on board, smashing his hatch coaming and flooding the cramped interior. Next, temptation came in the form of a three-masted barque bound for Liverpool, whose captain offered to take *Centennial* as deck cargo and relaunch her on the other side, saying nothing about the mid-ocean pickup. On July 16 he spoke the brig *Maggie*

Gander and sailed in company with her for a few hours until the next gale parted them. He then unshipped his mast, lashed it down on deck, and awaited the onslaught. Later that afternoon *Centennial* was capsized by a breaking crest, remaining inverted for some twenty minutes with Johnson hanging on to her flat bilges for dear life. When he finally managed to right her, and bail her out, he found he had lost his squaresail and paraffin stove, and that all his food and bedding was soaked. He carried on—what else could he do?

On August 7 he begged bread and fresh water from the brig *Alfredon*, and on the 9th obtained his position from the ship *Prince Lombardo*. He was then about fifty miles from the south Irish coast. He stood on, and on the 10th saw land for the first time: the Welsh coast near Milford Haven. Since the wind was against him, he landed at Abercastle, forty six days out of Shag Harbour. After a brief rest ashore, he left on August 12, arriving off Holyhead on the 16th, and at Liverpool on the 17th.

Apparently Johnson did very little to publicize this feat. He returned home, later became the owner of a Grand Banks fishing schooner, and died in 1930, aged eighty-three. Hardship, it would seem, does not prevent one from reaching a ripe old age (remember Brendan). Extraordinary adventure, apparently, is of no consequence to anybody else unless it is well written up and adequately publicized (remember Selkirk?).

Yet in spite of this, Johnson apparently acquired some recognition, since he was thereafter always known as 'Centennial'. And the word went round and inspired others: 'If Centennial Johnson could do it', they invariably replied, when questioned, 'then I don't see why I shouldn't have a crack at it'. 'It' covered a multitude of boating endeavours on many different seas and oceans, but 'it' probably meant and still means just one thing: in the end, against every advice to the contrary, the greatest adventure of all is to set yourself a task, no matter how impossible it appears, and to do your utmost to achieve success against all the many odds which inevitably will be set against you, and you alone.

Teamwork no doubt is a fine concept as instilled in all youngsters while they are at school, but the ability of any team is dependent on its weakest link, which is the one big flaw. Every loner, each singlehander, no doubt also discovers flaws within himself, but these he must control or circumvent, since he has to make do for himself or go under. The absolute knowledge of self-reliance could therefore be of greater benefit to mankind than sloppy team-spirit exhortations churned out by those who have little or no personal knowledge of survival against odds. In the sport of yachting, Centennial Johnson was the first man to prove that this philosophy could achieve startling results; the subsequent development of singlehanded voyaging owes much to him, and also to the eccentric Middleton, and to the more publicized MacGregor and McMullen, for showing what could be done.

The year 1876, then, marked the beginning of an ever-increasing number of small boats and yachts setting forth on some enterprise or another. Most of them carried two or more crew, and therefore do not concern us in this investigation of singlehanders—although I must continue to mention some, since they help us to recognize the various solo achievements. For example, the very next voyage in 1877 was the first to be made by a married couple: Thomas and Joanna Crapo, who crossed the Atlantic from the west in the 19 ft *New Bedford*; I will have more to say about Joanna in a separate chapter about women singlehanders. Then, in 1878, the two Andrews brothers crossed in their 20 ft *Nautilus*, and some years later William Andrews was beaten by 'Si' Lawlor in the first-ever singlehanded transatlantic race, discussed in the next chapter.

Then again, since I am British, I should mention Frederick Norman and George P Thomas, who were not only the first of British nationality to cross the Atlantic in a small boat, but in the smallest so far to make the attempt, and the *smallest boat ever* from east to west by the northern route—a record which still stands—since they were also the first to make a double crossing. In 1880 they sailed from Gloucester to Cowes in forty-six days; in 1881, from London to Halifax in seventy-nine days. Their boat, the cutter rigged *Little Western* (16′ × 6′), had been specially built in 1879 for the voyage at a cost of £100.

However, for the most part Americans, or immigrants to America who became naturalized, were responsible for nearly all the small boat transocean voyages until at least the turn of the century. There were very few exceptions. In 1881 John Traynor (British) and Ivar Olsen (Norwegian) sailed the cutter *City of Bath* (18′ × 5′) from Kennebec River, Maine to Newfoundland; and from there to Falmouth in Cornwall in the shortest time to date, twenty-six days; but not the fastest time, because the distance covered was only 2000 miles. This little dory cost £150 to build and equip for the voyage, and following the McMullen principle there was absolutely no profit motive (unlike *Little Western*, which did well on exhibitions).

Not only were the Americans conquering the Atlantic almost unopposed, but the Pacific, too, was being tackled. In 1877 a remarkable character who was probably no less eccentric than the English gentleman E E Middleton Esq. was so impressed by Alfred Johnson's solo Atlantic voyage that he decided to go one better. He would be the first to sail alone and non-stop across the greatest ocean of all: the Pacifc.

Bernard Gilboy, a native of Buffalo, New York (though his parents were both Irish immigrants), made his first singlehanded transpacific voyage from British Columbia to Hawaii in fifty days. Neither the dimensions nor the name of his boat are known, although it was described by Gilboy as 'open'. Even the year, 1877, is unconfirmed, and is entirely supposition on my part since he was listed as a seaman aboard the steamer *Pelican* the year before—which was when Johnson crossed the Atlantic.

In 1882, at a cost of $400, he had built and provisioned the flush-decked, schooner rigged, clinker double-ender *Pacific* (18′ × 6′). On August 18, a month short of his thirtieth birthday, with five months' provisions on board (which included many luxuries such as tinned roast chicken, roast salmon, roast beef, boned pig's trotters, etc) and 140 gallons of water, he set sail with the intention of making Australia in one hop. He succeeded—but only after he had capsized twice and lost his mainmast, compass and chronometer; after *Pacific* had been rammed by a swordfish; after he had lost his log when crashing across a reef; after losing his rudder and finally his steering oar; after he had entirely run out of food and was forced to eat sea birds, and barnacles from his boat's bottom ... On January 29, 1883, exhausted by hunger, he was picked up by the schooner *Alfred Vittery* only 160 miles from his objective, Australia, having sailed and drifted more than 7000 miles in 162 days—non-stop!

So Centennial Johnson's feat was directly responsible for Gilboy's gallant attempts at conquering the Pacific—and who will quibble at the 160 miles which he did not sail to Sandy Cape and thus complete his second voyage? These two men, therefore, were undoubtedly those most responsible for arousing interest in the possibilities of singlehanded transocean voyages which, ninety years later, spawned an explosion of international interest in the now-famous transatlantic races.

5
The Singlehanded Transatlantic Races

The surprising fact about those first recorded singlehanded transocean voyages is that when the Atlantic and the Pacific were finally conquered (and the gap between the two solo 'firsts' was only a year or so), fifteen years passed before the Atlantic was again beaten by a singlehander from west to east, and fifty-one years before the Pacific was crossed against the sun—although the first solo circumnavigator, Joshua Slocum, sailing westabout, crossed it in 1896. But in both the quoted cases, *two* vessels departed during the same year, with the same object in mind: in 1891 Josia W 'Si' Lawlor and William A 'Bill' Andrews raced across the Atlantic; in 1932 Fred Rebel and Edward Miles departed from Australia and Japan respectively for America, and probably never knew in their lifetimes about this extraordinary coincidence.

But first, I will deal with the singlehanded transatlantic races—abbreviated later to STR, STAR, or OSTAR.

Just as yacht racing in Britain began in 1661 directly *Mary* had some opposition, so did two Americans evolve singlehanded transocean racing 230 years later when each became jealous of the other's popularity as a result of previous small boat exploits. The first transatlantic race took place in 1891, the second in 1892; there was also a third in 1901. The common denominator of all three was a high-browed, straight-nosed, moustachioed, rather grim looking individual: William A Andrews.

I don't know exactly when he was born, but it must have been around 1840. No doubt he knew something about the small boat adventurers I have already described, because in an interview in 1901 he was reported as saying: 'I had heard that a man named Johnson had crossed the ferry in 1876 in a small boat twenty feet in length, and since success had crowned his effort I saw no reason why I should not emulate his achievement.'

He was referring to his first voyage in 1878. He had been employed in a piano factory at Boston, but trade was bad and so he decided to start his own business, for he was a mechanic and a piano-builder by profession. Before taking this step, however, he was determined to visit the *Exposition Universelle* which was being celebrated in Paris in that year.

> The chief point I had to consider was how to get across, because I was not in a position to pay for my passage in the ordinary way. I mentioned the matter to my brother Walter, who immediately approved of the idea, and we at once completed our arrangements for our novel journey. I went down to Gloucester to the shipbuilder who had constructed Johnson's boat and ordered a similar craft sixteen feet in length. But the boatbuilder refused to build it less than twenty feet in length, as he was apprehensive of its being sufficiently safe. Seeing argument was useless I let him have his own way, and in five days the boat, which we called the *Nautilus*, was delivered to us. We set out from Boston, Massachusetts on June 8,1878. A huge crowd gathered to wish us *bon voyage*, and a large fleet of boats accompanied us for a short distance. We did not get far before we encountered our first disaster in the shape of a broken compass. We put back into Beverley, and I seized the opportunity of waiting for the readjustment of the compass to have the sleeping accommodation rendered more comfortable. My bunk was only 11 inches in width by 8 inches high, and I had to lie upon my side with the hatch open. This was due to the centreboard of the boat. The advantage of having such a small bunk is that when the vessel pitches and rolls there is no danger of being hurled out of the berth. The boat was not ballasted, and is the only craft that has ever accomplished such a journey under such conditions.[From the various passages quoted in Chapter 4, we know that this assessment by Andrews is incorrect.]

When the alterations had been made and the compass rearranged we made a fresh start. The weather was frightful, the wind blowing from the northeast, and no vessel would put to sea. Nothing daunted, and chafing at the delay already caused, we decided to put off, though everything augered an unsuccessful passage. Fortunately, however, the weather moderated when we got well out to sea.

When we dropped out of sight of land that night we vaguely wondered whether we should ever see it again. I had never been at sea before; I had no ideas of navigation, and naturally had never taken an observation of the sun. Our plight seemed hopeless and the attempt foolhardy. But we resolved to continue the journey, come what might. We took the observation of the sun whenever possible, and settled upon our course as well as we could. During the trip we spoke thirty-seven vessels, and by their aid could rectify any errors that we had made in our calculations regarding longitude and latitude. In spite of our deficient knowledge in this respect we struck the Bishop's Rock off the Scilly Islands, and for which we had been making our way in a fog, so that we had not erred much in our observations. We made up to the Scilly Islands, and the following day entered the English Channel and ran into Penzance, being under the impression that it was Falmouth. We experienced a difficult time in these waters. A northeast gale was blowing and we got into the Lizard Race—a terror of all mariners. The sea was running high, and the tide was sweeping us along backwards against the wind at a speed of nine miles an hour. We finally landed at Mullion Cove, and right glad we were for the opportunity to get ashore to stretch our limbs after being cramped up in the narrow confines of our little boat for forty-five days. We subsequently made our way to Havre, thence to Paris. After the exhibition we returned to England, where we stayed for several months exhibiting our boat, since the episode had aroused considerable attention. We then returned to the States, and shortly after our arrival home my brother was taken ill and succumbed to the malady.

I have quoted Andrews at some length because his approach to the venture is interesting when compared with the expertise and gadgetry which is considered so necessary these days. After the death of his brother Andrews continued to sail alone, but eleven years passed before his next Atlantic crossing, when once again the object was to visit the Paris Exhibition. This time, however, he was determined to be more professional in making money out of the trip.

He had *Mermaid* built, lateen rigged as *Nautilus* but this time only 15 ft long. Then he met an enthusiastic showman who wanted him to take his boat on a short tour before he set sail; this promoter insisted on changing the name of the little boat to *Dark Secret*.

At first I was not in favour [Andrews said]. It sounded ominous. But he was adamant. At last I told him I would only consent to so do for £100, thinking that the mention of such a high figure would preclude further insistence upon his part. To my surprise, however, he closed with me immediately. He also made another contract with me that I should tour with him with my boat for forty-seven weeks at a weekly remuneration of £20 and expenses.

I started from the pier at Point of Pines near Boston on June 17, 1889. The advantage of starting from Boston is that the journey is some 250 miles shorter, and one enters the Gulf Stream much earlier, the warmth of which is very appreciable, while it carries you along at a splendid pace. More than 28,000 people witnessed my departure, and as I had contracted to receive a percentage of the pier receipts for this event I netted a further £280. On this occasion I had the boat constructed with a hollow keel in which I intended to carry my water, but before I sailed I was supplied with Hygeia water in bottles. I then admitted sea water into the keel to ballast the boat. I had scarcely got clear of the land, however, when I experienced rough weather. A strong head wind was blowing and the seas were running very high. Still I pushed on steadily, hoping that the elements would become more propitious. But my anticipations were doomed to disappointment, for the weather became worse. I was buffeted about for sixty-two days and made no progress. In fact I was driven back. After I had been out for a month I spoke a vessel which informed me that I was only 150 miles off Boston. This news depressed me, but at the end of another fortnight when I spoke another vessel I was informed that I was only 100 miles out.

To aggravate matters my water gave out, and when I spoke a Norwegian barque a few days later I was glad in one sense of the word to get on board and to sit down to a hearty meal in the captain's room after two months' subsistence upon canned food.

When I reached America I learned that a Mr J Lawlor had successfully crossed over to France in a small boat, and had created a tremendous sensation.* This put me upon my mettle, and I resolved to make another try. I ordered another boat, the *Mermaid,* the same dimensions as the *Dark Secret.* While the boat was being built I met Lawlor and we agreed to race across the Atlantic for £1000 and a silver cup. His craft, *Sea Serpent,* was of the same length as mine, but rigged differently with a spritsail.

This was the first transatlantic race with small boats, and it aroused widespread interest. We started together from the Ocean Pier near Boston on June 17, 1891 just before nightfall, amid the huzzas of a large concourse of people. The weather was extremely rough. When we got away from land we decided upon our respective courses. Lawlor went north and I went south. Lawlor, however, must have changed course soon after leaving me, since I passed his sprit, which he had cast adrift. By this I saw that he was taking the same course as I projected. My theories in this direction were further substantiated when I spoke a vessel which informed me that they had passed Lawlor 'all well' three days before, and about a thousand miles (*sic*) ahead of me. As for myself, I encountered successive disasters. My boat capsized seven times, and on one occasion I was clinging to her bottom for half an hour. She was wrongly constructed. Lawlor had fitted his boat with a lead keel, so that if she capsized she would right herself immediately. My boat would not do this. I had to right her the best way I could. To make matters worse, five days after we set out I ran into a cyclone. The seas were so heavy that my boat was practically crippled. All my stores were damaged and my water was lost. Under these circumstances I decided to seek

*This was not a singlehanded sporting voyage, but in the tradition of *Red, White and Blue.* Lawlor's father, a boatbuilder, had constructed an 'uncapsizable and unsinkable' vessel called, appropriately, *Neversink* (40′ × 12′), and designed by the inventor F L Norton. Crewed by two American seamen and skippered by Si, she departed from New York on May 11, 1889 and arrived safely at Le Havre on June 28, when she was displayed in the Paris Exhibition of that year. In this manner, Lawlor acquired the reputation of being a great navigator—which Andrews at this stage certainly was not!

assistance from a passing steamer. I sighted the *Elbruz*, of Antwerp, and was taken on board. I proceeded with her to Antwerp, and sold my boat for a handsome sum to a syndicate of showmen. I then went to London and met Lawlor, who had safely made a place near Land's End, and then went to Portsmouth, having accomplished the journey in about forty-three days. [Actually 45.]

Although the last two attempts to cross the 'Ferry' had resulted in failure, Captain Andrews (as he termed himself) was by no means daunted, and wagered Lawlor that he would cross in thirty days. Si Lawlor also decided to endeavour to lower his own record, and for this purpose both competitors set to work to construct special vessels. Andrews christened his *Flying Dutch-man*, an auspicious name. Lawlor called his the *Christopher Columbus*. In an interview Andrews said:

> While my vessel was being built I was commissioned by the manufacturers of a well known domestic commodity to name the vessel the *Sapolio* and to undertake the trip on their behalf. I communicated to Lawlor my projected course, which was to be from Cape Race to Queenstown, a distance of only 1800 miles. Lawlor replied that his designs were precisely the same. But I suddenly learned that a celebration was to be held in Spain, in honour of Columbus, since the year was the four-hundredth anniversary of [his] discovery of America. It then suddenly occurred to me that it would create a sensation if I were to sail for the very town from which Columbus had set out in his expedition. The *Sapolio* was 14 ft 6 in overall, with a beam of 5 ft and a depth of 2 ft 3 in. She was collapsible. I had 39 sq ft in the sails. Lawlor, anxious to reap primary honours, started on his trip before I was ready, but he never reached his destination, for he was never heard of again. However, I did not know then about his tragic end, and so I was not deterred from my purpose; I set out on July 20, 1892. On this occasion Fortune was kind to me. The weather was all that could be desired, and the wind was so favourable that I reached the Azores in thirty days, a distance of 2500 miles. Profiting by my previous experience with the *Mermaid*, I had had a lead keel provided to the *Sapolio*, and it was a gigantic success. From the Azores I proceeded to Portugal,

made my way up the coast, and finally reached the Spanish town of Huelva and Palos after twenty-six days.

Contrary to what most writers have quoted in the past, Andrews seems to have sailed his canvas-sided collapsible boat across the Atlantic on this occasion in sixty-nine days, counting his stopover in the Azores, and not the eighty-four days generally reported. 'I averaged in fair weather about 100 miles every twenty-four hours, which is by no means a despicable daily run considering the size of the boat,' said Andrews.

Somewhat cheered by his overwhelming success in Spain, he decided to make another attempt in 1898—this time in a 13 ft gaff sloop, complete with jackyard topsail and a boom longer than the boat (total sail area 108 sq ft), which he named *Phantom Ship*. He sailed from Atlantic City on August 24, but the boat leaked, his food was ruined by salt water, and he was forced to abandon the attempt. He was picked up on September 27.

In the early 1960s I read about somebody who intended to *swim* alone across the Atlantic. His idea, apparently, was to tow a small raft on which food and water could be carried, and on which he could sleep at night. Even this plan was not quite so crazy as Andrews' next 'shipmate', Professor Miller, who intended to *walk* from Atlantic City to England.

Andrews rebuilt *Phantom Ship* (which had been, and still was, a fold-up boat, only 4 in thick when stowed), reducing her overall length by 12 in and re-naming her *Doree*. He agreed to accompany Miller as 'safety vessel'. Andrews also designed Miller's two 'shoe-boats', which resembled model canoes 5 ft long, with serrated flat bottoms. Needless to say, the attempt failed at the start. Andrews, however, went on.

> I think this was the most remarkable trip I have undertaken, since, although I did not accomplish my object, I passed through a succession of experiences such as I never wish to meet with again. I was supplied with a large stock of Saratoga water, a natural effervescent drink. I sailed on June 17, 1899 from Atlantic City and made very fair progress. The weather was hot and for some inexplicable reason I felt peculiarly drowsy. I had never experienced the sensation before. When I commenced writing my log, for the first few minutes the writing was quite bold and distinct, but it soon resolved itself into an unintelligible scrawl and I

would fall asleep. A first I attributed the peculiarity to the heat. I took my observations in the usual manner, and conjectured that I was keeping a good course. One day when I fell in with a vessel, wishing to rectify any errors that I might possibly have made, I asked the captain for the longitude. He gave it to me, and you can judge of my surprise when I found that his observation was three days ahead of mine. That is to say, I had travelled three days farther than I imagined. I thought he must be in error. I asked him the date of the month. 'July 1st', he retorted. 'You must be wrong', I replied: 'it is only June 27th'. He quickly dissipated my doubt upon this point, and I was at my wits' end to account for such a flagrant error in my calculations. I continued my journey in a dazed condition. One day when it was abnormally hot I laid down in my bunk. Immediately I experienced a strange feeling of asphyxiation. I jumped up in alarm. Thinking it must be fancy on my part I once more lay down, and the same curious sensation overtook me. I thereupon sought to discover the reason for this peculiarity. It was not a difficult search, for I found that the cork stoppers to my bottles of Saratoga water had shrunk under the influence of the intense heat, and that the carbonic acid gas had escaped and had collected in the bottom of the boat. This was the solution of my curious drowsy feeling. I could not account for my error in longitude. I must have been unconscious for those three days, since I never had the slightest recollection of them. Since I had now discarded my water I kept a sharp lookout for a vessel to replenish my supply. The first ship I spoke was bound for Liverpool, where I eventually landed.

During the course of all this to-ing and fro-ing by Bill Andrews (who certainly made himself quite a deal of money in the process), three other singlehanders, apart from the unfortunate Si Lawlor, crossed the Atlantic.

The first of these, Rudolph Frietsch, a Finn aged thirty-four, is somewhat mysterious. It is known that he sailed from New York on August 5, 1894 in the 40 ft schooner *Nina*, and that on September 5 he engaged a pilot for £3 to help him sail his large yacht into port (another contestant in the McMullen 'heavily sparred yacht' stakes?) and to place her 'in a suitable berth for exhibition at Queenstown.' Whether he made any money out of this showing to the public is not known, but two months later (on November 7) Lloyds recorded that during a hurricane she 'was driven on the rocks in Ettrick Bay, at the north end of the Island of Bute, and will probably become a total wreck.'

The other transatlantic singlehander during the nineties was Joshua Slocum, who crossed from Yarmouth, Nova Scotia to Fayal in the Azores during 1895 in eighteen days, and from there to Gibraltar in eleven days, a total of less than twenty-nine days—a remarkably fast passage! Cunning old Josh, then aged fifty-one, with all the wisdom of forty-three years' experience afloat, set sail on August 25 and arrived in Pernambuco harbour on October 5, forty days out of Gibraltar. A double crossing in a yacht as heavily sparred as McMullen's *Orion*, and at speeds which are not easy to beat, even to this day. It was at Pernambuco that Slocum shortened *Spray*'s boom—*not* because the gear was too heavy for him to handle, but to repair the damage caused by a gybe when he was fleeing from Moroccan pirates shortly after leaving Gibraltar.

But more about this famous singlehander in due course. In connection with the transatlantic races, we still have the final contestant of that period to consider: Howard Blackburn.

The story of how Blackburn lost all his frostbitten fingers, half of each thumb, two toes from the left foot, and three toes and a heel from the right, after losing sight of the Banks fishing schooner *Grace L Fears*, the mother ship, while dory fishing over the Burgeo Bank south of Newfoundland in a violent snowstorm during the year 1883, has been told many times before. Then aged twenty-three, he and his dorymate Tom Welch tried to row something like sixty or more miles to the mainland in atrocious conditions. In the early stages Blackburn had lost his mittens while bailing, and it was then that he made the frightful decision of freezing his hands around the looms of the oars so that if the mother ship found them he would not be seen as a useless doryman, unable to help himself. Welch died during the second night at sea, but Blackburn continued to row towards Newfoundland until eventually he located the small, impoverished hamlet of Little River on the sixth night of this frightful epic of survival. (But think of all those other unremembered whalers and fishermen over the centuries.) The settlers, although in desperate straits themselves, lacking food (except for a little flour, cornmeal and dried codfish) and clothing (the children stumbled barefoot on the icy ground), saved his life: three months later, when he was moved

79

to the town of Burgeo, the doctor there said he could do no more for him than the settlers had done already.

Here, then, we have a seaman cut from the same jib as Johnson and Slocum. Lawlor, son of a boatbuilder, was perhaps of a somewhat different cloth, but certainly his approach to seafaring was not as casual as the publicity seeking Andrews.

Blackburn opened a tobacco shop in Gloucester in 1884, finally purchasing the property and turning it into a saloon in 1889. He had married an Irish girl, Theresa Lally, in 1886, who bore him a son in 1887 who, through a mistake, was accidentally killed by his nurse. Theresa was unable to have any more children, and Blackburn was heartbroken. But in spite of his personal physical handicap, and the trials of his shorebound life, he prospered.

Then into his life exploded the Klondike—the biggest gold strike since 1849. Blackburn organized the Gloucester Mining Company, bought the fishing schooner *Hattie I Phillips* for $2500 (110 ft overall, 96 registered tons), and sailed for San Francisco with sixteen fortune hunters—probably in the same manner as J M Crenston had done forty-nine years before. The year was 1897, and Slocum had preceded them through the Magellan Straits twenty-two months before—they liked it no more than he had. They arrived at 'Frisco 129 days out of Gloucester, including a six day stop at Punta Arenas: a very fast passage indeed.

Of the adventures of the *Hattie I Phillips* and the Gloucester Mining Company it is enough to say that most of the participants returned in due course, much wiser men once the sparkle of gold nuggets had faded forever from their eyes. Of them all, Blackburn had been the first to see the flaws, and he had abandoned the expedition in 'Frisco and returned to Gloucester by train in June 1898. He had learned one important personal lesson: his pride, his temper and his singlemindedness of purpose were such that he would always be considerably better off if he relied only upon himself. He was, he knew at last, a natural-born singlehander.

Just as Andrews and Gilboy had been inspired by Johnson, Blackburn, who already knew the full story of the Gloucester fisherman, was suddenly encouraged by his feat to emulate his solo voyage. Johnson was now master of his own fishing schooner, sailing out of Gloucester; Blackburn would soon be master of his own yacht, sailing towards the British Isles.

There is no doubt that Blackburn knew exactly what he was attempting. Since he had visited the western seaboard of America, it is more than likely that he had heard about Gilboy too. He was fully aware that Johnson, Lawlor, Andrews, Frietsch and Slocum had crossed the Atlantic singlehanded—indeed, that Slocum had traversed this long and wide ocean three times, since he had arrived back in Newport, Rhode Island the previous year, on June 27, 1898, after completing the first singlehanded circumnavigation. Howard Blackburn's voyages were not stunts, nor were they money-making promotions; even McMullen might have approved.

He had built the clipper bowed *Great Western* (30′ × 8′6″), a little sister of the small fishing boat used on that part of the coast and known as a Gloucester sloop. She was without doubt the prettiest of all the solo voyagers' craft to date.

He bore away from East Gloucester Yacht Club on June 17, 1899 to the sound of an estimated 10,000 cheering well-wishers; on the same day, almost at the same hour, Bill Andrews was sailing out from Atlantic City in his 12 ft *Doree* to the cheers of an estimated 30,000 onlookers, many of whom had paid for the privilege. The professional amateur and the amateur professional were very nearly engaged in a STR without realizing it: this is probably the reason why it has been suggested that a race may actually have been arranged between them, although there is no evidence whatsoever to support this view.

Blackburn had a tough time on this first small boat voyage since his dory survival experience seventeen years before. His right leg, which he had injured in 'Frisco, began to swell and throb with pain; he became feverish and couldn't eat or sleep. But he hung on, and in due course the swelling subsided. He ran into unexpected easterlies and had to beat to windward for hundreds of miles; he chafed in many flat calms. As a result of all these vicissitudes he made a very slow passage: sixty days to the Isles of Scilly, which he sighted on August 16. Two days later he tied up alongside the pilot boat on station off Portishead up the British Channel, and the next day, with a pilot on board, sailed up the River Severn to Sharpness, from where he was towed along the sixteen mile canal to Gloucester by the steam yacht *Sabrina*. Gloucester to Gloucester: a friendship was established as messages from mayor to mayor were exchanged. Thus ended the first officially approved, singlehanded, goodwill voyage, although it was later extended when Blackburn sailed *Great Western* round to London, where he stayed for six weeks. Here he sold his transocean yacht to R K Braine, the brother of Gloucester's mayor, and it is possible that *Great Western* still survives in some forgotten British creek.

E.S.H.—F

The next year, 1900, Blackburn built the *Great Republic*—a smaller yacht this time, because he had some difficulty in handling *Great Western*. She measured 25 ft long, with a 7 ft beam. He sailed and tuned her, alone, throughout that season.

On New Year's Day in 1901 he issued a challenge through the press for a singlehanded race across the Atlantic to Lisbon, Portugal, commencing in mid-June. He proposed a stake of $100 per entry (or more if competitors required it), half to be deposited with the Commodore of the East Gloucester Yacht Club by March 1 as evidence of good faith, and the balance to be paid by May. Rules were negligible: no boat to exceed 30 ft overall; each must be sailed singlehanded; no tows or pickups by other vessels. A number of stunters, money-promoters and cranks showed interest, but none appeared too eager to back their ideas with hard cash. The yacht race aspect seemingly had no appeal to anybody.

Bill Andrews, however, was certainly interested, although he had problems of his own which were causing him some misgivings. At the age of sixty-one he had married the woman who had nursed him back to health after his disastrous voyage in 1899. (His previous wife had died some years before.) His immediate response to Blackburn's challenge was a reply to the press that he was certainly interested, and that he would enter a boat of only 12 ft overall, 'Since my experience with the *Doree* had convinced me that a craft of these dimensions is splendidly adapted to such an expedition.' But then, just as he had changed his mind before the race with Lawlor and opted for a Spanish finishing line instead of Irish, now he decided that there would be more publicity value in a 'honeymoon cruise' than in just another transatlantic race. It would seem that he had not heard of Thomas and Joanna Crapo—although theirs had certainly not been a honeymoon cruise, since they had been married for five years.

So instead of a 12 footer, he resurrected his 15 ft *Dark Secret*, which had been taken on board the Norwegian ship that had rescued him in 1889 and had since been used frequently by Andrews to illustrate his many lectures. That the boat was in a bad state after twelve years of shore ill-treatment did not bother him. Slocum was equally slap-happy with *Spray*, and I have known many Thames barge skippers who sailed continually with doubtful gear and leaky craft, seemingly without a care for the consequences. In a last minute rush, long after Blackburn had set off, Andrews and his bride departed from Atlantic City for Spain.

82

They spoke one ship, the steamer *Durango*, whose captain reported that 'the poor woman looked as though she had been bleached, so white was she from seasickness or fright'. They were never seen again. I suspect *Dark Secret* was the weak link though, not Mrs Andrews.

The challenge for the third STR had been made, and although there had been no takers Blackburn decided to go anyway and try for a record passage. He was then forty-two years old, over six feet tall, and weighed 256 lbs: tough, gnarled, self-confident— although wind and sea had done something towards rounding off the jagged, granite chips which had so often brought him near to financial disaster in the past. Now he was a 'good man', popular with everybody, well disposed towards benevolent charities.

He set forth to the rousing cheers of thousands of spectators, drowned only momentarily by the report of the East Gloucester Yacht Club starting gun, fired from aboard the Commodore's yacht, at 1415 on June 9, 1901. There followed the usual deep-water adventures, the monotony relieved this time by some savage attacks against his ship by several swordfish, which he discouraged by dropping coils of rope on them as they came at the hull. Wind, rain, squalls, calm, storms, wet, cold—it is only a matter of facing them all, day after day, week after week, until in due course, by the very nature of the endeavour, you must reach the other side, or fail. He made Cape Espichel, thirty miles south of the entrance to the River Tagus which leads to Lisbon, on July 17 at 1700: a thirty-eight day record-breaking passage.

So ended the first batch of three singlehanded transatlantic races—all from west to east. The fourth race, which was the first from east to west, did not take place until many years later, in 1957. It was entirely unsponsored, and only briefly reported in the press; but there was at stake one dollar, and so for accuracy I should enclose brief details.

The contestants were Edward Allcard (British), who had already crossed the Atlantic in both directions alone (1949 and 1950) and with a companion (1952), versus Peter Tangvald (American) sailing the 21 ton (TM) *Windflower* to Los Angeles. (I should add that this was the commencement of Allcard's singlehanded corcumnavigation, which he has only recently completed: in 1973, after sixteen years, he returned to English Harbour, Antigua and so tied the knot—setting a duration record for cruising alone.)

On November 20, 1957 both singlehanders started their race

from where they were moored in Las Palmas harbour in the Canary Islands to English Harbour, Antigua in the Leeward Islands. Allcard's 36 ft Bermudan ketch *Sea Wanderer* was quite a bit smaller than Tangvald's 45 ft gaff yawl, but the physical disadvantages of handling the heavier gear of the larger boat would help to offset the longer waterline advantage. So the two yachts were not so dissimilar as to make the winner a foregone conclusion.

Tangvald described this fourth STR in a letter to John Pflieger, then Commodore of the Slocum Society Sailing Club.

I met Allcard in Las Palmas, and we decided to race across the Atlantic for $1. My ship is three feet longer than his on the waterline, nine feet longer overall, and obviously faster. But I had only my fore-and-aft rig with no twin spinnakers like he had, and my engine was not working (I had drained all the gas from the tank, being afraid of fire). So we figured it would be only fair to allow *Sea Wanderer* the use of her engine as a handicap for my longer boat. To save wear and tear on my gaff mainsail, I unbent it and made the crossing under a large trisail.

During the first half of the trip the winds were light and Allcard headed me, thanks to his engine; but about halfway the weather changed, with three days of very heavy wind which would push *Windflower* at surfing speed in a foam of water. I wrote in my log: 'Sure glad to see in *Sailing Directions* that it never blows more than Force 7, otherwise I would have estimated it at Force 9!' The third day the wind moderated to about Force 5, and I covered about 125–150 m.p.d. I arrived December 21st, and my thrill at seeing an island over my bow when the sun came up, and sailing into beautiful English Harbour not knowing whether I had won or lost, is hard to describe. I declined all offers of help to tie up to the dock, as I was afraid to be disqualified, but I had no trouble doing it under sail. (The bet's condition was first man across, tied up to the dock, singlehanded.) Two days later Allcard came in under power looking very surprised and disappointed to see me there.

After my thirty-one day crossing I was more rested and in better shape than when I started. Not for one minute did I ever regret having left my well paid job in Los Angeles and starting on this venture. I am a graduate engineer, born in Norway 33 years ago and now a naturalized American.

Whether or not it was this episode which sparked off the idea which Blondie Haslar later developed, in conjunction with the London *Sunday Observer* (now *The Observer*) and the American Slocum Society, into the now famous event known as the Observer Royal Western Yacht Club Singlehanded Transatlantic Race, I can only say that Richard Gordon McCloskey, who in 1955 had formed the Slocum Society 'to encourage long-distance voyages on small yachts, and keep records of such passages', wrote to me in 1957 asking my opinion about whether it would be a good idea 'to promote a singlehanded or a two-crew race, or perhaps a cruise in company, across the Atlantic.' Being anti-sport minded myself, and never particularly appreciative of winners of races, I immediately plumped for the cruising angle, adding 'but why in company'. It seemed to me then, and it still does, that the main object of going to sea in a small boat is to get away from everybody for a while—not to encourage a sort of general social get-together. 'Besides', I added cynically in my letter, 'if an event such as this becomes popular—which I very much doubt—it won't be long before the Atlantic is cluttered from shore to shore with floating hoardings advertising just about anything. As Frederick Fenger once remarked: "Yots? *Oh, stretch my luff*! Of course some slew-minded galoots will call 'em yots . . . !" But if they *race* them transatlantic, they won't remain in the yacht category for very long. Bloody floating ads, promoted and sponsored by money-greedy Big Businesses, are *not*, in my opinion, yachts.' I wrote a good deal more, but that reveals the gist of my feelings on the subject.

Well, I was wrong—and right!

The first OSTAR (or fifth STR) was barely sponsored by anybody except the *Sunday Observer*, who laid on a very quiet, eve-of-the-race dinner at Pedro's Restaurant in Plymouth on June 10, 1960. A couple of dozen people dined that night, including the five competitors: Blondie Haslar, David Lewis, Francis Chichester, Val Howells (all British), and the Frenchman, Jean Lacombe. It was a come-as-you-are affair, and rather subdued. I sensed the same tension which I had known on many occasions during the war on a night before a particularly dicey raid against the enemy, but the competitors did not attempt to relieve the strain as we had: with a good booze-up after the meal. So four went to their bunks, while Blondie Haslar, John Pflieger, Chris Brasher (the *Observer* representative on the spot) and I propped the bar at the Royal Western Yacht Club and argued the pros and cons of sponsorship versus freelance adventure.

After our lonely battle during the desperate voyage round the east coast in my barge *John & Mary* only three years before, I condemned the intrusion of a newspaper actually promoting danger. 'This is neither true sport nor real adventure,' I argued. 'It is merely a tenuous extension of publicity which will ensure that the name of a newspaper is repeated more often.' I lost the argument, although I believe I scored some points with Haslar and Pflieger; Brasher, with his past experiences of teamwork in sport, naturally could not accept my ideas on the subject, although he did agree on one thing: if the race became an annual event, sponsorship of individuals would become inevitable, because the cost would be too much for most people to bear.

Forty days later, Chichester arrived in New York, followed by Haslar (in forty-eight days), Lewis (fifty-six), Howells (sixty-three), Lacombe (seventy-four).

I do not propose to go into details of these now famous races, which have taken place every four years since the first of the series in 1960. Regrettably, nobody has a chance of winning outright now unless he is adequately sponsored and able to commission a specially-designed boat. Five singlehanders completed the 1960 race, fourteen the 1964 race, nineteen the 1968 race, and forty the 1972 race.

There was very nearly another race in 1971–2 which, if it had been completed, would certainly have been as spontaneous as the Allcard versus Tangvald affair.

In 1971 Mr B Goodwige, landlord of the *Anchor Blue*, a pub at the well known yachting centre of Bosham in Sussex, offered a barrel of beer to the winner of a singlehanded transatlantic race from the home port to the West Indies Windward Island of Barbados. There were three contestants, using identical craft of the Hunter 19 class (19′ × 6′2″ × 3′3″) designed by Oliver J Lee. The race started on December 19, 1971 to the great joy of enthusiastic journalists, but to the considerable detriment of the participants. Alan Gick capsized, and failed to right his Hunter until the mast broke and most of his gear was lost or destroyed. Geoffrey Cath capsized seven times before he reached Lisbon, on one occasion completing an 'Eskimo roll' (a similar capsize happened to Marcel Bardiaux). On two other occasions Cath was separated from his boat when it flipped over. Nigel Harman, the third entry in this rather foolhardy affair, left a few days after the others and had an exciting sail to Vigo, five and a half days out of Falmouth: a fast passage. He then went on to Lisbon, where he and Cath decided to abandon the race.

Foolhardy, perhaps, for mid-December is not a particularly good time to cross the Bay of Biscay; but I must admit I like the spirit of the thing far more than the tedious predictability of more organized events.

It would be unfair if I did not mention that the disasters which accrued during this brief competition cannot really be blamed on the design of the boat. On June 17, 1972 David Blagden left Plymouth in *Willing Griffin*, a specially altered Hunter 19, taking part in the fourth OSTAR, and arrived at Newport, Rhode Island on August 8 after a very successful Atlantic crossing. The jacket blurb on his subsequent book *Very Willing Griffin* (Peter Davies, 1973) is not literally true, but the story certainly vindicates the seaworthiness of the design. This is how the blurb put it: 'The sloop *Willing Griffin* (17 ft 3 in on the waterline, less than a ton) was the smallest boat ever to take part in the Singlehanded Transatlantic Race, one of the toughest races in the world.'

She was, of course, the smallest to take part in any OSTAR, but certainly not the smallest in all the singlehanded transatlantic races.

6
Early and Solo
Women Voyagers

The generally all-male participation in singlehanded small boat adventuring tends to make the subject less of a romance of the sea and much more of a battle against odds—which, among other things, is purely a device to demonstrate manhood. Add a snippet of the opposite sex and in theory one should be well on the correct road back to romance, but it seldom, if ever, seems to work out like that. Singlehanders, whether male or female, are in a class of their own which involves a form of sexlessness which can only be named 'one-track-mindedness'. That a woman should wish to run away to the miseries and vicissitudes—and only very, very sparsely, joy—which is all that the sea can offer, is really no more of a mystery than why a man does the same thing. There have been attempts to explain this strange desire, but I do not subscribe to any that I have read. It is quite impossible to generalize, or even offer alternative psychological explanations: in my opinion each and every genuine singlehander has quite independent and different reasons for doing what he or she does, and they are no more able to describe their emotions than they could explain the precise brainwork involved which enables them to survive when others would perish.

As in the case of male singlehanders, it is of interest to consider the earlier small boat transocean voyages made by women—and it is important to remember the point which I made with regards to Brendan, Magellan, Drake, et al: that *all* vessels in those days were small by current standards.

It is impossible to state with any certainty who was the first woman to cross an ocean, but the first *recorded* long distance passage was that made by the wife of one Thorodd, both of whom were part of a crew of twenty-six Norse under the captaincy of a man named Snaebjorn Hog in AD 980. This information comes from the *Landnamabok*, a contemporary Icelandic history which lists almost every man and woman of importance who lived in Iceland during its occupation by the Vikings, whose immigration, which began in AD 874, had increased the population to an estimated 40,000 by 930. This means that many women must already have voyaged long distances from the British Isles and especially Ireland, and from Norway, to Iceland, usually in large curraghs or in Norwegian *knorrir*, which were the cargo-carrying versions of the better known Viking longships.

The captain of a *knorr* was generally the owner. In this case, Snaebjorn shared joint ownership with one Rolf the Redsander. As a result of a blood-feud (the Norse were continually fighting among themselves), Snaebjorn was forced to flee from Iceland, and since it was considered unwise to return to Norway they sailed westwards to Greenland, which had been discovered by Gunnbjorn Ulf Dragesson over a century before (ca AD 877). After wintering ashore Rolf and a close friend, Styrbjorn, killed Thorodd (who was Snaebjorn's foster-father), and then managed successfully to murder Snaebjorn. With their family troubles sorted out, Rolf then set sail direct for Halgoland in the north of Norway, from whence he eventually returned to Iceland—where he and Styrbjorn were promptly killed by one Sveinung, who in turn was slain by Thorbjorn . . . But there we must leave them to their bloody feuds, having learned briefly that Mrs Thorodd sailed from Greenland to Norway in the year 981, and was therefore the first European woman known to cross an ocean in a small boat.

The first woman to sail around the world, however, comes into an altogether different category. When Captain Louis Antoine de Bougainville led the first French circumnavigation in 1766–9, sailing westabout via the Magellan Straits, his flagship *La Boudeuse* was supported by a storeship *Étoile*, which spent two months of 1767 exploring the dangerous channels of Tierra del Fuego, north of Cape Horn. Baré, servant to Philibert de Commerçon, botanist on this ship, was a great help during this difficult period and certainly qualified as a competent explorer, undergoing all the hardships and perils of sea and shore. Not until the two ships were together in Otaheite (Tahiti) was Baré's true sex discovered by the 'noble savages', who were not quite the fools most Europeans took them to be. 'She', their chief declared with certainty, 'is a woman!' And so she was discovered. She confessed, we are told, in tears—which I doubt. Gallantly, de Bougainville allowed her to continue with the expedition (she was then aged twenty-seven), and thus she became the first woman to circumnavigate the world, and the toast of France.

I cannot believe this story as it stands. Baré undoubtedly made the voyage, but to suggest that Frenchmen could not tell the difference between sexes is going a little too far. Similarly, I have never accepted the 'facts' about Mary Read and Anne Bonny, who were tried for piracy on November 28, 1720. They existed all right, but the romantic nonsense written about them must belong to the same poetic licence as the 'discovery' of Baré. There were no private bathrooms, toilets, or heads on ships in those days; how could a woman escape discovery?

We are told that Anne Bonny's father, a lawyer, had emigrated to Carolina where he built up a good practice and eventually purchased some plantations. Then Anne's mother died, and she became heiress to a considerable fortune. But she eloped with a pirate, James Bonny, who took her to New Providence where she met Woodes Rogers. Her husband then turned informer, which upset Anne as she liked pirates, so she took up with one Jack Rackham, known as 'Calico Jack', although seemingly she was perfectly happy to share the hammock of anyone who cared to ask.

Now although we have already seen many coincidences within the microcosm of small boat adventurers, I cannot help feeling that Anne's meeting with Mary Read is just a little too glib. Mary was supposed to have fought as a man in Flanders until the Treaty of Ryswick brought temporary peace. After this military career she married a fellow trooper, and when he died sailed to the West Indies. She was then middle aged, but nevertheless she somehow managed to join Calico Jack's crew. This occurred while Anne was away in Cuba having a baby (which she promptly abandoned), but when she returned she was rather taken by this 'handsome' new crew member, and she revealed her sex to 'him'. Jack Rackham was furious at her infidelity (I don't believe it: Anne slept with anybody) and threatened to kill them both. Then, in true Hollywood style, Mary revealed her hidden secret.

Well, it all seems very unlikely, and we can thank Captain Charles Johnson (Chapter 3) for the melodramatic details. Giving evidence at the trial, however, witnesses were unromantically terse: '. . . dressed in men's jackets and long trousers, and a kerchief tied about their heads'; their sex was recognized 'by the largeness of their breasts' (so how was it that the pirates didn't spot them); '. . . they cursed and swore at the men to murder me'; '. . . they were both very profligate, cursing and swearing much, and very ready and willing to do anything.' Two French witnesses who had been captives of Jack Rackham, John Besneck and Peter Cornelian, made it perfectly clear why *they* had not been fooled. 'When we saw any vessel, gave chase, or attacked, they wore men's clothes; at all other times they wore women's clothes.' None of the evidence was contested, but when the two women were asked if there was any reason why they should not be hanged like their fellow pirates, they 'pleaded their bellies' and the court misguidedly reprieved them.

The stories of Baré and the two British pirate women have been told many times, in varying ways. I have drawn attention to them for one reason: to show that when women become involved with such masculine pursuits as sailoring, truth is often bound to get distorted.

I am not against Women's Lib, but I do wish the distaff side would apply some common sense when they begin to think about adventuring at sea in small boats. I receive many letters each year from women who, on paper, are determined to 'get away from it all' by 'following my husband into a completely new life afloat'; or 'by showing that a woman is just as capable as a man' when they decide to go it alone. Of course journalists thrive on this kind of copy, but the general rule concerning individual pre-promotions of daring is that they are as unlikely to succeed as most of the suicide attempts which are carefully arranged as public exhibitions in order to arouse sympathy—and thereby publicity, and perhaps hard cash.

However, Mrs Joanna Crapo, the first woman to cross an ocean in a small boat, did not come into this category. In 1877 her husband had decided to sail alone to England, presumably to challenge the first singlehanded crossing by Alfred Johnson the year before, since he designed and had built an almost identical boat which he named *New Bedford*. Her dimensions were 19'7" × 6'2" (5 in shorter, 4 in more beam) and the rig a ketch with leg o'mutton, triangular sails on 21 ft 6 in and 21 ft masts, instead of the gaff cutter rig favoured by Johnson for *Centennial*. *New Bedford* was the first small boat to cross the Atlantic with what is now called a Bermudan rig. Why his wife suddenly decided to

91

join him on this impossibly small vessel has never, to my knowledge, been revealed.

Joanna, a Scot, had married Thomas Crapo in 1872 at Marseilles, when he was first mate of the brig *Myronus*, and it has been variously reported that she had sailed with him on several occasions, and that she had learned navigation and could have become a female Master Mariner. This, once again, I doubt, since throughout the voyage in *New Bedford* she did absolutely nothing towards handling the boat, and only just about managed to feed her man with warmed food when the weather allowed.

For the tiny, double ended boat was flush-decked, with only one small hatch for the helmsman and another amidships where Joanna could stretch her legs. The headroom below was only 2 ft 6 in! Try to imagine the appalling difficulties of living below in that cramped space in the voluminous female clothing of the day. We do not know exactly what she wore for the voyage, but we can be sure that it was quite unsuitable. Even modern fabrics would soon absorb salt air and water, and become permanently damp and miserable to wear in such conditions; Joanna's main contribution to the crossing would seem to be that she managed to survive.

Most of the food was tinned or pre-cooked. If this sounds attractive, don't be misled: 90 lbs of ship's biscuit and 75 lbs of tinned meat defines the bulk of the stores, plus some tea, coffee, sugar—and 100 gallons of water in five breakers. What 'cooking' Joanna contrived was carried out over a small kerosene lamp which Thomas had to hold between his feet, 'so the motion of the boat will have no effect upon it, as no one knows when it will explode.' The wick smoked, the lamp spilt oil, the heat was insufficient to do more than warm the food and mull the drink— and poor Joanna had to cope with this for fifty-one wearying days.

With all the stores, plus ballast, there was very little room for the crew. Thomas, like so many husbands who take their wives to sea in small boats, proudly told how she suffered even in sleep. 'Mrs Crapo's feet rested on the water kegs and should she desire to turn over she would first have to rise.' He does not bother to mention what Joanna had to say, but perhaps she was better trained and more obedient to her spouse than the modern seagoing wench.

They sailed from New Bedford, Massachusetts to Vineyard Haven, and from there to Chatham on Cape Cod where they were met by 'a multitude of people'. Crapo did not miss the opportunity for selling a large number of photographs of the boat. From there, after some repairs and alterations by a painter and carpenter (and *New Bedford* had only just been launched), they set off on June 2, 1877. They had the usual type of transatlantic crossing: speaking many ships, surviving several gales, wallowing in fog and calms, meeting some whales, nearly getting run down . . .

Joanna was entirely responsible for the latter catastrophe since her weary husband had left her on watch while he rested during the night of July 2, and she, unfortunately, also fell asleep; she awoke to find a steamship bearing down on them, and only prompt action by Thomas saved their lives. I wonder what he said to her? Since this was only a week after they had spent three-quarters of an hour on board the German barque *Amphitrite* (when they were twenty-six days out of Chatham), where they had a meal and wrote two letters, one suspects that Joanna's resistance to the continual strain was weakening rapidly.

Crapo did not once allow her to touch the helm. Instead, he fought his way across the Atlantic by sailing *New Bedford* for nineteen or twenty hours out of every twenty-four, and heaving-to when he slept. He was a firm believer in the use of a drogue or sea anchor in a storm, and on one occasion he remained on the foredeck and 'played' his ship to the drogue continuously for eighteen hours because the seas were particularly steep and dangerous.

Finally, they staggered into the little Cornish fishing port of Newlyn on July 21, at 2300, after a last-ditch effort by Thomas who had remained at the helm for seventy-two hours. Nobody saw them arrive. They tied up alongside a fishing boat, lit their oil stove to brew up a celebrating drink—and did not wake until daylight had broken.

Well, Joanna was the first, and I think she certainly earned this distinction, even if she did nothing towards the handling of the boat. *New Bedford* was taken by rail to London and exhibited at Alexander Palace for six weeks; then the boat and crew made a tour of Britain before going back to America. Further tours and exhibitions in the United States made Thomas enough money to buy a schooner and start trading. In 1895 he was able to buy a larger vessel, the brig *Manson*, but he lost her three years later. Another schooner, *Gustie Wilson*, he lost almost immediately in a gale off Cape Hatteras. In May 1899, presumably in an attempt to raise more capital after these losses, he set forth from Newport, Rhode Island towards Cuba in a 9 ft boat, *Volunteer.* His body was found off Charleston, South Carolina some time later. Of Joanna, nothing more is known.

Scarcely any women attempted such voyages in the nineteenth century, although it must not be thought that none went to sea. An appreciable number accompanied their husbands, who were captains of whalers, clippers, packet ships, Pacific traders, and so on. Many became famous when, through one reason or another, they took charge of the ship, or replaced an incompetent or ill mate. But unfortunately these heroines are not within the scope of this book.

We have already seen how Bill Andrews tried his honeymoon cruise stunt in 1901, and I must admit that I have always felt sympathetic towards this particular girl. Rightly or wrongly, I assume that this was a case when the man demanded the presence of the woman as a necessary adjunct to his promotion plans; generally it's a female who requests, pleads or demands to be taken (as Joanna Crapo must have done), in which case she does not warrant much sympathy if things go wrong.

Another unfortunate woman, who I believe was the very first to achieve a singlehanded voyage—even though it was entirely accidental, and completely involuntary—did receive a great deal of sympathy, including a personal tribute from Queen Victoria herself. She was a sixty year old Shetlander, Elizabeth 'Betty' Mouat, who in 1886 survived a solo, nine day, 400 mile voyage in the 50 ft smack *Columbine.*

This sailing packet was captained by James Jamieson, aged twenty-eight, with Jeremiah Smith as mate and Oliver Smith as deckhand, running a regular service between Lerwick and the southern parts of Shetland, with a fortnightly mail and provisions journey to the remote Fair Isle. On January 30, 1886 Betty Mouat was taken aboard at Grutness for a passage to Lerwick to see the doctor there, as earlier she had suffered a stroke which had slightly paralysed an arm and a leg. She was the only passenger.

Within half an hour of *Columbine*'s departure, watchers on the shore noticed that she was making very heavy weather: continually luffing, bearing away and then coming up into the wind again. Other spectators further up the coast spotted the ship's boat, with two men rowing desperately to get through the offshore breakers at the mouth of a rock-strewn channel. Their story, when eventually they landed, was soon told. They had left about noon, when the wind was already blowing so strongly from the SSE that the skipper had double-reefed the mainsail. In the rising gale, violent rolling caused by the heavy seas had parted the main-sheet. The captain and mate were hurriedly reeving a new one, when they were flung overboard to port by a particularly vicious wave. Both had hold of the mainsheet, but the mate managed to claw back aboard. He and the deckhand immediately launched the ship's boat in order to rescue the captain, leaving the sails as they were (double-reefed but unsheeted main; foresail and jib flogging). They failed to find the captain, and within minutes the mate realized that it would be impossible to row back to the *Columbine*, which was sailing rapidly away from them, and that they would be extremely lucky if they could save themselves in those atrocious seas. Well, their luck was in, but they were completely exhausted when they staggered ashore from their half-filled boat.

Betty had been below in the tiny cabin during all this panic. She had tried to climb the ladder to see what was happening but had slipped and fallen. When eventually she recovered and looked out on deck she discovered that she was alone. The helmsmanless *Columbine* was pitching and rolling so violently that all she could do was sit on the cabin sole, hang on —and pray. After a time, an even heavier lurch crashed the ladder down: she was now a prisoner in the cabin, with only a quart bottle of milk and two biscuits which she had brought with her for what she had thought would be a three hour voyage.

Eventually, after nine days and eight nights of almost ceaseless storm, *Columbine* sailed herself—much of the time backwards— to the Norwegian coast, where she grounded on the rock-strewn island shore of Lepsoe, twelve miles north of the fishing town of Aalesund. Here, at last, Betty was rescued by the islanders.

It would seem from the detailed information supplied by Roderick Grant in his book *The Lone Voyage of Betty Mouat* (Impulse Books,1973), that she became very nearly an interna-tional heroine. Her story was published in full in the *New York Herald*, surprisingly, and it appeared in many Scottish and English newspapers and magazines, which one would expect. Certainly Betty came out of the affair rather well, living for a time in Edinburgh where she was visited by a great many people who seem to have regarded her as something akin to a miracle worker, or even a prophetess. Promoters, speculators and the like tried to buy her services, but she refused them all, although she accepted a gift of nearly £400 which was raised by subscripton and included a cheque for £20 from Queen Victoria. Then she returned to her home in the Shetlands and surprisingly, in view of her earlier stroke and her undoubted sufferings on board *Colum-bine*, lived for a further thirty-two years, dying peacefully in her bed on February 6, 1918 at the age of ninety-three.

Although Betty crossed 400 miles of storm-lashed seas alone in a boat, for obvious reasons we cannot consider her the first woman to sail singlehanded across an ocean. So who was?

In the late spring of 1941, in company with a Canadian pilot, Flying Officer C F 'Much' Turner, I spent an enjoyable few days relaxing from war flying strain at the small port of Salcombe on the south Devon coast. On one of these days, Much and I walked westwards round the promontories of Bolt Tail and Bolt Head to the tiny fishing village of Hope Cove. This, in itself, became quite an adventure, because we became involved with a shroud of ghosts who, we learned later, had been a band of smugglers massacred by Revenue men more than a century before. When we arrived in Hope Cove we were arrested by the Home Guard as leaders of a German invasion... but enough of that.

One old-timer recognized our ghost story as being entirely true, and since he had been a man of the sea in his younger days it was not long before he and I were swapping yarns. I told him that I had originally joined the RAF in order to save enough money to buy a boat in which I hoped to sail around the world, and that I had bought my yacht and all I was waiting for was the war to end.

And then he told me about the woman who had put into Hope Cove in 1903, '... or was it 1904? Cain't tell 'ee fer sure, but I reckon 'twas around forty year ago.' He'd discovered her and her small boat at sunrise, not in the tiny harbour but nosed into the gully of the stream that flows into the sea on the east side of the village under the cliffs, 'jest a-standing there, top o'the tide, holdin' the painter, an' lookin' up at the cottages.' She was young, 'no more'n a score'n half', her face was tanned, her black hair was tangled and salt-corroded, and she wore an ankle-length grey dress: 'grey t'was, not white gorn dirty, but grey'. She had been alone—he was quite sure of this—alone, and not too sure of herself. What was she doing there? Where had she come from?

She evaded his questions at first, requesting only some help in refilling a water cask from the stream which chuckled around their feet. Although it meant missing the tide and that day's fishing, he took her home to his cottage, his wife and (as far as I can remember) their three children. There, after she had washed her sore body ('sea sores all over, me wife told me afterwards: chapped an' broken-skinned an' chafed an' the like'), and eaten, she told them her name was Gladys Gradely, and that she had come all the way from America, alone, in the tiny clinker-built lugger which now lay at the mouth of the creek. Of course they didn't believe her: no fisherman would have accepted such an unlikely story—and yet afterwards, when his wife told him about her poor, damaged skin, he was not so sure that her story was untrue. 'Two months she said she'd bin at sea: two months out of one of they American ports—tho' I've forgotten the name.'

The boat, he told me, was about an 18 footer, lug-rigged, with a small cuddy for'ard under a raised deck, but otherwise flush-decked except for a tiny cockpit.

And that was about all he could remember of her.

She sailed on the evening tide, up Channel, and that was the last they heard of her. Some of the other fisherfolk watched her departure, and the general consensus was that she was competent enough at handling a boat. 'She gave us a photo of her and she', the old man told me, but when I went with him to his home he could not find it. His wife had been long dead, and his children departed, and the little cottage, though it was clean enough, resembled a museum of Victorian bric-a-brac. He asked for my address, which I gave him, for he promised to send the evidence on to me when he found it; I must admit that I promptly forgot all about this little episode because of the more puzzling and much greater adventure with the ghostly smugglers, et al.

So it was something of a shock from the forgotten past when, about eight months later, I found a re-addressed letter in my mail. Written with a very shaky hand, it told me merely that he—the **old fisherman** at Hope Cove—had found the photo, and here it was, and that he hoped I was as well as could be expected in these terrible times. Alas, I've forgotten his name; and both his letter and the photo I had to consign to the deep after *John & Mary* staggered into the shelter of Walton Backwaters in the teeth of a nor'easterly gale in 1957 with her interior awash.

But in my mind I can still see the photo of this first-ever transatlantic female singlehander—for that is what I believe she was. It was a sepia print, mounted on thickish card which had once been folded, so it was badly creased; also, unfortunately, the sepia had faded, so that the highlights all but merged with each other. Yet there she was, in a black dress this time, with her black hair piled on top of her head and her face very white, with deep-sunk eye sockets. She looked consumptive—as did most people in the photographs of those days. Her black-gloved right hand rested on the stemhead of—presumably—her transocean boat, which reached just below her shoulder. There was no forestay, or a sign of any fittings—not even a fairlead; the stem was straight, the planking clinker, and there was no name on the bow. The photographer had only been interested in the woman, and he had not even included part of the mast in his composition. Across the bottom was her signature, Gladys Gradely—or that is what I translated the scrawl to mean.

There is a sequel of sorts to this strange tale, just another of those many weird coincidences which seem to occur within the microcosm of the small boat world. In 1954 the French maritime writer Jean Merrien published the English translation of *Lonely Voyagers*, in which he described many transocean passages in various craft. In the Appendix, listing these trips in date order, he noted: 'Honeymoon voyage, 1902: Mr and Mrs Bradley (USA?), Nova Scotia to Dover, arrived July 21, thence to Anvers; 16 ft boat, no other details available.' Similarly, in Humphrey Barton's *Atlantic Adventurers*, exactly the same sparse information is noted, with the brief addition: 'Left Dover bound for Antwerp and London.' Now Bradley and Gradely are not so very different in spelling or form, and since my fisherman informant was quite positive that Gladys had crossed the Atlantic alone, it is possible that the male half of the crew was invented because nobody believed that Gladys had sailed alone. For example, many years passed before the first singlehanded crossing of the Atlantic was entirely believed, simply because Alfred Johnson admitted that he had been offered a 'lift'; it is very easy to put ideas into disbelievers' heads!

So I plump for Gladys as being the first woman to cross the Atlantic singlehanded, and I hope that one day I may receive further confirmation. On the meagre evidence quoted, however, this declaration is entirely a personal matter; in all fairness to the next, and totally proven, solo woman crossing, I must leave this claim in abeyance.

About fifty years passed before the next voyage of any distance was made by a woman alone in a small boat. During this long period yachts of all sizes, with crews ranging from several down to one person, crossed and re-crossed all the oceans and seas of the world, creating many 'firsts', 'fastests', and other records. Frequently women formed part of these crews, but it was not until 1934–7 that Edith Strout became the first woman to circumnavigate in a two-crew yacht, the skipper being her husband Roger. These two Americans sailed westabout, from Jacksonville in Florida to New York via the Panama Canal, Torres Straits and the Cape of Good Hope, in an exact copy of Slocum's *Spray* which they had built, and named *Igdrasil*. For this 'first' they received the first of six Blue Water Medal Awards by the Cruising Club of America to husband-and-wife combinations, in four of which the wife was the sole crew.

But back to the singlehanders. On May 18, 1952 Ann Davison set forth from Plymouth for America in her tiny sloop *Felicity Ann* (23′ × 7′6″ × 4′6″). She made a leisurely journey at first, calling at Douarnenez, Vigo, Gibraltar, Casablanca and finally Las Palmas in the Canary Islands. After several weeks' stay she left the Canaries on November 20th, reaching the West Indies island of Dominica after a lengthy passage of sixty-five days for the crossing of about 3000 miles. In due course she sailed, still alone, from there to English Harbour, Antigua, where she spent some time refitting *Felicity Ann* (or 'Sweet F A', as she sometimes affectionately called her floating home). Then she went north, calling at many of the islands on the way, to Nassau, to Miami—and finally to New York, via the Intracoastal Waterway which provides a sheltered passage virtually all the way up the eastern seaboard.

Sheltered passage? I can only suggest you read her book *My Ship is So Small* and find out the details for yourself. Ann arrived in New York on November 23, 1953.

No doubt resulting from this experience, she decided six years later to make a singlehanded circular tour of the eastern half of America in a 17 ft twin-outboard cabin cruiser, which she named *Gemini*, by repeating her trip up the Intracoastal, going through the Erie Canal into the Great Lakes, and across to Chicago. From there she could connect by canal with the Illinois River, and so into the Mississippi and all the way to New Orleans. A harbour-hopping cruise around the northeast coast of the Gulf of Mexico, and so back to Miami, would tie the knot of this unique 6000 mile trip.

Apparently she was not aware that fifty-eight years before, between May 18, 1902 and February 20, 1903, her equally famous singlehanded transatlantic predecessor Howard Blackburn had sailed *Great Republic* from Gloucester, Massachusetts to

Chicago, via New York and the Erie Canal, through to Columbus, Ohio on a tributary of the Mississippi. From here he had sent his boat by rail to Mobile, Alabama because the river level was too low for safe pilotage, but from Mobile he had sailed to Key West on the southern tip of Florida where, six miles offshore, *Great Republic* had been stranded on a sand bar and badly damaged. He had managed to salvage her, but he had been forced to sell because he couldn't spare the time while she was repaired. He had then continued his voyage by rowing 400 miles to Jacksonville in a 12 ft dinghy which he christened *Laura C Strong.*

Blackburn did not 'tie the knot', but then he had sailed and rowed while Ann had motored. These two voyages, however, reveal yet another surprising coincidence which is not generally realized.

Twelve years later, a thirty-five year old American, Sharon Sites, made a 2480 mile solo Pacific crossing from Marina Del Rey in California (reputed to be the largest marina in the world, mooring 6000 yachts) to Hawaii, in her Folkboat sloop *Sea Sharp* (25' × 9' × 3'6"), sailing on June 12 and arriving July 21, 1965, taking thirty-nine days, four and a half hours. Four years later, having married her former sailing instructor Al Adams and cruised to Hawaii with him in the 31 ft ketch *Maria* (which was owned by a diabetic who only just survived the voyage; he sold the boat), Sharon Sites Adams sailed *Sea Sharp II* (30'10" × 9'9" × 3'9" ketch) non-stop and alone on a delivery voyage she had arranged with an American-owned boatyard in Japan, from Yokohama to San Diego, a distance across the Pacific of 5911 miles in seventy-five days (May 12–July 25, 1969), averaging 78·8 m.p.d. This remains, at the time of writing, an unbroken time and distance record for any singlehanded woman.

Close to her heels in the same year 1969, but this time in the Atlantic, one of my trimaran customers, German-born Ingeborg von Heister, sailed her British built, Piver designed (35' × 20' × 2'6") ketch rigged Lodestar class tri *Ultima Ratio* from Las Palmas to Barbados in thirty-three days. The next year, 1970, she returned via Bermuda to the Azores in thirty days, and from thence to Gibraltar in sixteen days. Ingeborg thereby became the first woman to cross the Atlantic in both directions singlehanded.

And so, quite suddenly, nearly a thousand years after the wife of Thorodd had been the first woman on record to make a double ocean crossing of a sort, the Atlantic *and* the Pacific were crossed in both directions by two women within a few months, and quite unbeknown to each other. Once again another extraordinary coincidence, and just one more of those moments when one cannot resist admitting that it's a small world, and that there's nothing new under the sun—even though clichés sound somewhat trite in these circumstances.

All the girls needed to do now was the usual polishing up: subdividing these first 'firsts' into secondary 'firsts'.

On June 12, 1971 Nicolette Milnes Walker sailed from Dale in southwest Wales in her fibreglass sloop *Aziz* (30′ × 8′), and arrived at Newport, Rhode Island on July 26, having covered 3400 miles non-stop at an average speed of 76·5 m.p.d. Since she followed the southern route, going south of the Azores before proceeding westwards, I cannot really see much difference between her non-stop westward crossing and those of Ann Davison and Ingeborg von Heister. If Nicolette had taken the northern route, she would have been more original, but I really don't think she added very much to what had already been accomplished before by the other two singlehanded women. In her book *When I Put Out to Sea* she admits that Ann Davison had pioneered the voyage, adding that she had done it via Spain and the Canary Islands as though this made it much easier. (Actually, it makes the voyage longer, and adds to the hazards.) Obviously she had not heard of von Heister, nor of any other long distance singlehanded voyages by women. So I think the opening statement in her book is somewhat misleading; she says, 'Because I was the only woman to have succeeded in crossing the Atlantic non-stop and alone, my arrival made a small splash in history.' Since Ann and Ingeborg also succeeded in crossing the Atlantic non-stop and alone, I cannot honestly see the validity of her claim. It would be more correct to record that she was the first woman to cross the Atlantic alone and non-stop from Britain by the southern route— which isn't quite the same thing, and is neither a time nor a distance solo record.

In the 1972 OSTAR the three women entrants all completed the course from Plymouth to Newport; two French and one Polish, their yachts and times are listed in Appendix 9. It is, perhaps, worth mentioning that the French also claimed that Marie-Claude Fauroux (who finished first of the three) was the first woman to sail singlehanded across the Atlantic.

The greatest 'first' that is left now for a woman to accomplish is a singlehanded circumnavigation. Whether it is westabout via Panama (the easier route), or rounding the Capes of Good Hope and Horn, running the easting down for endless weeks, or surmounting the Mount Everest of yacht cruising endeavour by doubling those same Capes westabout—some woman, one day, will have to be first, and those who follow will gradually improve on her initiative. And then, just as it has been with singlehanded male circumnavigators, all that will be left will be the 'fastest', the 'slowest', the 'youngest', the 'oldest'—and so on through the superlatives.

Bow and stern views of Slocum's famous *Spray*. The heaviness of the gear is particularly noticeable in the stern view.

Joshua Slocum

John Voss' Indian dugout canoe *Tilikum* in Oak Bay, Victoria BC in May 1901, just before she left on her incredible voyage. One of the very few survivors of the early days of small-boat adventuring, she is now preserved in the Maritime Museum at Victoria. She is probably the oldest 'yacht' in existence, being approximately 175 years old.

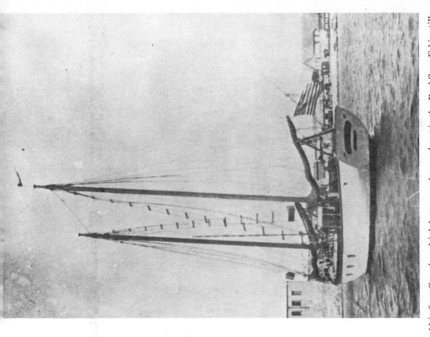

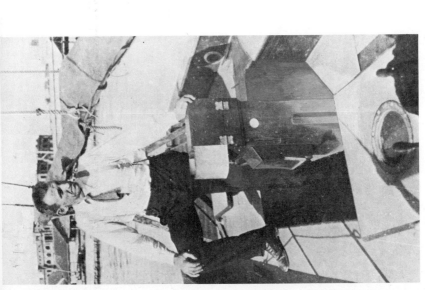

A rare photograph of Ed Miles, taken in 1929 on his fiftieth birthday, at Alexandria on board his first *Sturdy*, which later was burned out in the Red Sea. Ed is still the only man to have circumnavigated singlehanded eastabout via the Suez and Panama Canals.

Like Gerbault's *Firecrest*, *Legh II* (note change of spelling) was destroyed by those who wished to preserve her. Sailed by students of the National Nautical School from Buenos Aires towards Mar del Plata in August 1971, she was driven ashore in bad weather and almost totally wrecked.

Vito Dumas and *Lehg II*. The first man to sail round the world alone eastabout entirely in the Roaring Forties.

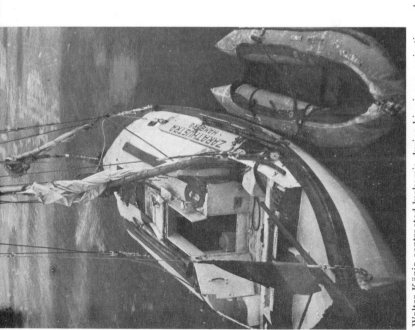

Walter König contracted luekemia during his circumnavigation and died on December 30, 1969 shortly after arriving home in Hamburg in his converted fibreglass lifeboat *Zarathustra*. Although it cannot be proved that his early death was entirely due to his ambition to complete a round-the-world voyage, it must stand as a lesson to those who follow.

Victress, the first multihull to be sailed around the world singlehanded. She held the fastest time to 'tie the knot' until she was beaten five years later by Alain Colas and his 70 ft trimaran *Manureva*.

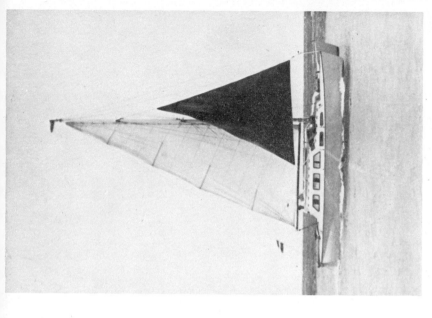

The first catamaran to circumnavigate singlehanded, 32 ft *Taboo* was designed in Britain by Erick J Manners and built in Australia by Austrian-born Wolf Hausner, who then went round westabout via the Panama Canal.

Sharon Sites Adams holds the record for women singlehanders: greatest distance (5911 miles) and longest period alone (seventy-five days) on her transpacific voyage in 1969 from Yokohama to San Diego in *Sea Sharp II.* Taken off California on the day before her arrival, this photograph makes it all look easy.

Clare Francis, who slipped across the Atlantic from Falmouth to Newport in 1973 without exciting any advance publicity, suggested to me that she was probably the smallest singlehander. Only 5 ft 2 in, weighing 105 lbs: I think she's right.

Although he was not the first Pole to circumnavigate alone, Krzysztof Baranowski set a so-far unbeaten record for monohulls of forty-five days from Hobart to the Horn in his beautiful *Polonez*.

After overcoming innumerable setbacks, Bill King became the first man to circumnavigate singlehanded via the five southernmost capes and return to his port of departure. *Galway Blazer II* was specially designed as a Cape Horner by Angus Primrose and cold-moulded in wood.

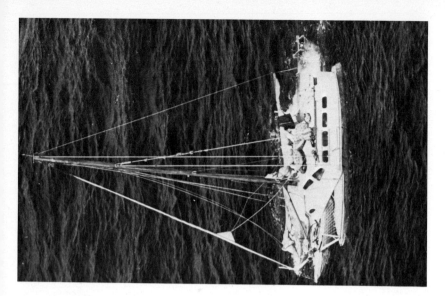

John Riding's incredible 12 ft *Sjö Äg* in San Diego. After successful transatlantic and transpacific crossings, he was lost when on passage from New Zealand towards Australia across the dangerous Tasman Sea.

The Piver-designed 30 ft trimaran *Clansman* was sailed singlehanded towards harbour when she was severely holed and full of water, thus demonstrating that modern multihulls rarely, if ever, sink, even when waterlogged.

Annette Wilde, the only woman to sail alone both ways across the Tasman Sea. Her 33 ft sloop *Valya* is built in ferrocement.

Kenichi Horie and *Mermaid III*, in which he became the first Japanese to circumnavigate singlehanded; he also beat Chay Blyth's nonstop westabout voyage against the Roaring Forties by seventeen days.

Japanese Hiroshi Aoki and *Ahodori II*—at 20 ft 9 in overall she is the smallest yacht to round Cape Horn under sail, and the second smallest to sail around the world.

The first Swedish circumnavigator, Göran Cederström and *Tua Tua* (1971–3). The first Swede to set out was Ulf Peterson in *Suzie II*, but his was a protracted voyage during 1968–74. Like the Germans, the Japanese, Poles and Italians, the Swedes are latecomers in singlehanded circumnavigation.

7
The Singlehanded Circumnavigators

And so at last we come to the dream which so many have sought to realize and so few have achieved. Yet I suspect that most of my readers will be surprised at how many have actually sailed alone around the world—and I will be the first to admit that even I was amazed when I compiled the list (Appendix 2), which I doubt is yet complete.

I often wonder what old Josh Slocum would make of it all were he still alive. 'The wonderful sea charmed me from the first,' he wrote. 'To face the elements is, to be sure, no light matter when the sea is in its grandest mood. You must then know the sea, and know that you know it, and not forget that it was made to be sailed over... The days passed happily with me wherever my ship sailed.' The man who wrote those words was not interested in breaking records.

Slocum rebuilt the old *Spray*, whose ancestry was and still is unknown (but remember *Bezan*?) at a cost of '$553.62 for materials and thirteen months of my own labour', and quite casually, it seems, he set out on what was to become the greatest 'first' ever achieved by a yachtsman. 'I spent a season in my new craft fishing on the coast, only to find that I had not the cunning properly to bait a hook. But at last the time arrived to weigh anchor and get to sea in earnest. I had resolved on a voyage around the world, and as the wind on the morning of April 24, 1895 was fair, at noon I weighed anchor, set sail, and filled away from Boston, where the *Spray* had been moored snugly all winter.'

How many singlehanders have succeeded in getting away from it all as easily as that, in three sentences? But the greatest are more often than not the last to be recognized. Slocum pulled off an amazing 'first', and wrote a wonderful book which probably has been more instrumental in promoting dreams of singlehanded small boat adventuring than any other ever published. Yet when his voyage was done, and his book written, seemingly he had passed the zenith of his life's purpose, for he achieved nothing else but an unhappy drift towards his nadir.

When, eight years after his circumnavigation, he was charged with attempting to violate a twelve year old girl on board *Spray*, and as a result spent forty-two days in jail, he was probably a long way past the point of no return. Rape was charged, but not committed; he pleaded guilty to indecent assault, and was discharged.

Three years later, on November 14, 1909 he sailed the *Spray* out of Vineyard Haven and into oblivion. Of course there were, and still are, theories, but it would seem that Slocum slowly deteriorated mentally, and in part physically, much as his beloved ship bore the scars of hard work, hard sailing and hard lying. Slocum was sixty-five, and the *Spray* a mere fifteen years since rebirth, yet probably both were equally unseaworthy. The captain suffered from occasional blackouts, possibly as a result of a blow on his head from a heaving line in 1896; the *Spray* suffered from casual, almost non-existent maintenance: she was 'considerably dozy' to quote just one comment. His intention had been to make another sensational voyage, up the Orinoco and down the Amazon; he had enjoyed fame, and yearned for further recognition. But his belief in his and his ship's ability to survive all the perils of the sea was misplaced; we shall never know which of them failed during this final battle against the elements.

There is a similar great sadness about many of the singlehanders who have achieved circumnavigations since Slocum. It would be nice to write only of adventure—of gallant in-fighting against natural odds—yet this is seldom true. The exploits of solo yachtsmen may make exciting reading for those who knew little or nothing about the subject, but the facts reveal much more of a laugh, clown—laugh pathos than a jolly tar or a happy wanderer.

There are, I think, two entirely different types of pathos among singlehanders. The first concerns finance, or generally the lack of it; the second is psychological. Sometimes, as with Slocum, the two merge. Add to these the seemingly carefree solo yachtsmen who proceed to break records without any apparent mental or physical impairment, and it would appear that every kind of person is covered. Unfortunately it is not as easy as that. How often during World War II had I seen the slow crumble of a happy-go-lucky pilot as insidious thinking of one sort or another burrowed through the caverns of his mind. One can never guess, nor can one ever prognosticate with any accuracy, what goes on, and what will happen in the mind of any natural loner.

I sold the 40 ft trimaran *Victress* to Nigel Tetley in 1963, and came to know him moderately well; nobody was more surprised than I when he was found hanged in a Kent wood a year or so after he became the first man to sail a multihull singlehanded around the world while competing in the *Sunday Times* Golden Globe Race of 1968–9. More often than not, the loner carries his mental secrets into his grave.

So the eccentric last years of Alexander Selkirk's life were more true to reality than Daniel Defoe's neat rounding-off of Robinson Crusoe's middle age. By declaring that there were many more adventures yet to recount, and thereby implying that Crusoe never grew really old, Defoe pen-carved a patient, heroic, benevolent image which probably is as memorable as one's mental picture of Jesus Christ. Fiction, it would seem, is much kinder than truth.

Truth is relentlessly harsh, and should destroy forever the happy thoughts of those who seek to escape from their responsibilities, of being the small cogs that they are in a gigantic machinery of civilization. John Voss, who like Slocum had captained many large sailing vessels, and who was the first to sail round the world *as a stunt*, spent his last years on a relative's ranch outside of Tracey, California, driving a jitney bus; he died there on February 27, 1922 at the age of seventy-one, of pneumonia and a dilated heart. For a man who had conceived the impossible idea of sailing a 38 ft Indian dugout canoe across three oceans, starting off in company with a Canadian journalist who knew absolutely nothing about the sea, with a promise of a mere $2500 reward if he succeeded, this is not at all the sort of ending one expects.*

*This is the popularly accepted version, based on the original publication of *The Venturesome Voyages of Captain Voss*, in Japan in 1913. Voss' Canadian companion, Norman Luxton, wrote an entirely different account of what happened, including a denial of any wager or reward, a statement that he (Luxton) had held a first mate's ticket since 1900 and was therefore a competent seaman, a

Very few singlehanders seem to have sailed away from the harsh, competitive world into simple happiness. The dream which evolves the ambition before the setting forth is seldom realized, or so it seems. Slocum sailed mainly because he had nothing else to do, and he loved the sea; Voss sailed because he was prepared to try any small boat venture if there was a chance of earning some dollars at the end of it. Both men, really, were no longer able to find employment which suited their independent tastes, and so they invented their own. Both expected far better pay for their efforts than they received.

It seems strange that right at the beginning of the long list of circumnavigators we can find one example of each of the types of men who followed.

Harry Pidgeon, the second true singlehanded circumnavigator, was undoubtedly one of the very few who found genuine happiness. Born on an Iowa farm in 1870, he did not even see the sea until he was eighteen, and although he had adventured in canoes on the Yukon, floated down the Mississippi on a raft, and eventually became a photographer, he never, as he put it, 'went out upon blue water'. In 1917 he began to build his *Islander*, from plans published by Thomas Fleming Day in *Rudder* magazine. His Seagoer class yawl cost him $1000 and eighteen months of hard work. He then tested her by sailing alone to Hawaii in twenty-six days, and returning to Los Angeles in forty-three, this time with crewman Earl Brooks. 'I had found the sea to be a great highway leading to wherever I wished to go,' Harry commented, and proceeded to plan a voyage around the world. Like Slocum, he was fifty-one when he set out in 1921; Voss had been fifty when he started.

His first circumnavigation was in every sense a huge success, although he was not overkeen with his own company: 'My

disbelief that the John Claus Voss who died at Tracey was the man who had sailed *Tilikum* nearly round the world, an assertion that Voss had told him that he was a Dane (not a German as is usually stated), a belief that Voss murdered the Tasmanian crewman Louis Begent who replaced Luxton when, through ill-health, he left the canoe at Suva (he claimed that Begent had not been washed overboard as described by Voss but had been killed in a drunken fight during the voyage from Suva to Australia), and that he, Luxton, had been solely responsible for conceiving the adventure and for payment for the vessel (a Siwash Indian canoe, estimated by the ancient Siwash crone who sold it for eighty silver dollars to be a century old and to have taken part in many battles on the west coast of British Columbia before being converted by Voss). The full story, edited by his daughter Eleanor Georgina Luxton, was published in 1971 by Gray's Publishing Ltd of Sidney, BC under the title *Tilikum: Luxton's Pacific Crossing*.

voyage was not undertaken for the joy of sailing alone. It was my way of seeing some interesting parts of the world'; and he added at the conclusion of his only book, *Around the World Single-handed*, 'Those days were the freest and happiest of my life.'

He enjoyed the experience so much that he more or less followed the same route again in 1932–7, thereby setting up the first double record, although I very much doubt if this occurred to him. When most people would think that he had done enough, he suddenly married (he was then over seventy), and after some short shakedown cruises with Margaret (who had been born at sea aboard a square-rigger commanded by her father), they set off from Los Angeles in July 1947, again in the trustworthy *Islander*, on Harry's third circumnavigation.

> When we sailed from Hawaii for Torres Straits [he wrote later], the old Pacific was in an even worse mood than when we had come to the Islands. When we sighted the Gilbert Islands we ran into heavy northwest winds and our main boom broke. After that we could set only a loose-footed staysail in place of the main. I had intended to pass through the Santa Cruz Islands, where I knew there was a good harbor, but the northwesterly gale drove us off to the southward. Then we held on for New Hebrides where there is a safe harbor on the south side of Santo Island. As we came alongside of Santo the wind came round dead ahead and we could not beat against it to the Segond Channel where the harbor is, so we ran back to Hog Harbor at the north end of the island. It was not a desirable place, but it was good shelter from the southerly wind then blowing. The day could not have been lovelier, only a faint breeze reached the place where we anchored, but the bottom was falling out of the barometer. The holding ground of sand patches and coral heads was not good. There was no sea in the harbor to speak of, but *Islander* began yawing in the wind. The chain rasped on the coral rock and parted. I tried to get under sail but the keel began bumping on the coral heads and we were driven ashore. The foremast tangled with a dead tree and showered us with falling branches, while the wind drove *Islander* with such force against a knee of rock that it smashed right through the bilge. We could step ashore, and in the wind and torrent of rain we began getting our belongings out of the water-filled hold . . .

Undeterred, Harry and Margaret returned to Los Angeles and built *Lakemba*, a Sea Bird class yawl (28′6″ × 8′6″), also designed by Day. She was launched in 1951 at San Pedro, but apart from some gentle offshore cruising they never had a chance to test her, or themselves, on a third world voyage. Harry Pidgeon died in 1954 at the age of eighty-four.

Alain Gerbault, the third singlehanded circumnavigator and the first non-American, was undoubtedly an eccentric even before he made the voyage. He shared with Greta Garbo the feeling that 'I vant to be alone'. Out of all the round-the-world yachts, *Firecrest* was probably the least suited to sail the seven seas: deep-draft, heavy keel, narrow-gutted, she was built in Rowhedge, Essex in 1892 as a Dixon Kemp-designed survivor of the ridiculous plank-on-edge designs which had been developed as a result of racing rules imposed by the Yacht Racing Association in Britain, who perhaps should have taken more notice of what E E Middleton had had to say.

With extraordinary mishandling the ill-treated *Firecrest* bounced and crashed around the world, finally reaching Le Havre on July 26, 1929, six and a quarter years after leaving Cannes. The French tend to become very emotional about this sort of adventure, and amid much *brouhaha* they awarded him the Cross of the Legion of Honour. Gerbault, having made a good deal of money from his books and the considerable publicity, donated his scarred yacht to the French Naval Academy at Brest. They were seemingly even slacker than the previous owner, for they succeeded in sinking *Firecrest* on July 30, 1931 on her very first voyage under their command: while being towed by a French Navy tug to Brest. Poor *Firecrest*!

Gerbault then built the *Alain Gerbault* (34′1½″ × 10′6″ × 5′7″), a Bermudan cutter (variously called by journalists and others *Firecrest II, La Blanche Fille de Soleil* and *Wanderer*), and left Marseilles to return to the lonely Pacific in February 1932. Nine years later he turned up at Dili in Portuguese Timor, ill with malaria. The hospital there treated him, and he attempted to continue his voyage towards Madagascar; the fever worsened, however, and he had to put back. He died in the same hospital on December 16, 1941. When the Japanese captured the island shortly afterwards, the *Alain Gerbault* disappeared. In 1947 Gerbault's body was moved to Bora Bora, a Pacific island that he particularly loved, and his tomb stands in the square at Vaitape.

The fourth singlehander was also eccentric, but in a diametrically opposite fashion to Gerbault. Ed Miles believed fervently in the Brotherhood of Man, and he was prepared to stake all his money on spreading this gospel. 'I am a small business man of Memphis', he declared in a pamphlet. 'I designed and built *Sturdy* myself, alone, with the help of one laborer for 3 weeks. I'm going round the world, going East, the harder way. If I make it, will be the first. It has been did 3 times going West.' He was not very literate.

Born in Newark, New Jersey on February 11, 1879, Miles had very little schooling and soon left to run away to sea. In time, he grew tired of this trade and joined up with a railroad gang, eventually becoming a contractor at Memphis. Immediately after World War I he drew up plans for and built a 53' × 16' 'mystery ship' from which he intended to preach his certainties of a second world war and recommend his Brotherhood. He launched her in the Mississippi, and after many disasters eventually arrived at New Orleans, where he reluctantly decided that the boat was all wrong for his serious intentions—so he went back to Memphis to make more money.

In May 1926 he began building *Sturdy* at Savannah, Georgia, and on August 31, 1928, after a shocking row with his wife, he departed from New York towards Gibraltar, which he made in forty-five days. On his fiftieth birthday he was in Alexandria, where he moored his yacht for eight months at the Royal Egyptian Yacht Club awaiting the correct season for sailing south through the Red Sea.* I was there in 1944 and saw a framed letter signed by him thanking the Officers for their hospitality.

Miles was the first circumnavigator to use an auxiliary engine, and it was because of this that he lost his first *Sturdy*. Three days south of Port Said—only 150 miles on his way—the petrol caught fire, and his yacht became a total loss. He decided to build again, but not in Egypt since he wanted an all-American boat (strange, considering his brotherhood idealism). He redesigned and built *Sturdy II* in Memphis, and at the same time got divorced. 'No fault of hers or mine,' he wrote, 'but the fixers had ended our married life for ever, and now they tole me they would ruin me.'

---

*It is interesting to note that Slocum had originally intended to take this route: 'Now, my course to Gibraltar had been taken with a view to proceed up the Mediterranean Sea, through the Suez Canal, down the Red Sea, and eastabout, instead of a western route which I finally adopted.' He was dissuaded 'by officers of vast experience in navigating these seas' who told him that longshore pirates were numerous on both coasts. In the event, he was chased by pirates from the Atlantic shores of Africa—which was when he broke *Spray*'s main boom.

He married a blonde who, he reckoned, could represent the Sisterhood aspect of his worldwide brotherhood campaign, and she could also meet him in every port and act as his secretary, companion, publicity agent and general dogsbody. He shipped *Sturdy II* (this time with a diesel engine) to Port Said, and arranged first class steamer, rail and air transport for his new secretary/wife, as befitted her position. Miles plugged away, visiting Ceylon, Singapore, Borneo, Hong Kong and Yokohama. His PR girl, however, abandoned him in India and returned to America, making a 5000 mile holiday detour at his expense.

Suddenly, Ed Miles' quiet persistence seems to ring a solitary bell. At every port he visited he had preached the same Brotherhood of Man theory, and he was convinced that he was on the right course to a better world. Shades of Brendan? or perhaps Magellan?

From Yokohama he made an engine-assisted passage towards Honolulu, an impossible-to-sail-direct route of 3500 miles. When he was only 520 miles from his destination the diesel packed up, but he had decided to make Honolulu and nothing would deter him: 'I had to make a big inverted U and travel 2440 miles in order to complete the 520 miles.' The passage took him fifty-eight days.

He lectured there for a month, and had considerable success. Then he sailed to San Francisco in eighteen days, went to Reno and divorced his blonde wife, returned to *Sturdy II* and sailed her to Los Angeles, San Diego and Matzalan in Mexico—where he married a dancer, still believing that a wife and/or secretary should be of considerable help to his peace mission. Continuing singlehanded, for he would not allow any of his wives actually to sail with him, he went through the Panama Canal, on to Cuba, and finally back to New York, where he arrived on June 17, 1932. The voyage, the boats, and all the many catastrophies had cost him $35,000. Now he was broke. Wife number three, Mrs Ida Kershbaum Miles, sued for divorce, and denied under oath that she already had a husband living, and that she had married only to gain entrance to the United States (she came to Mexico from Vienna). Miles refused to pay $20 per week alimony and went back to Memphis after selling his yacht for $1000, when the materials alone had cost him $6000 only two years before.

This eastabout world voyage is unique—even to this day nobody else has followed his route—but poor Ed reaped no benefit from it. If he had stuck to the story of his circimnavigation, there is no doubt that he would have become as famous as his predecessors. But he considered the sailing only as a means to an end, and Captain Edward Miles' International Brotherhood (which he incorporated in February 1933) was of much greater importance to him. Neither publishers nor newspaper or magazine editors were interested in his fight against racial and religious prejudices. Completely broke, he left Memphis for Chicago, and there worked at odd jobs, saving every penny for 'his work'.

In 1944 he ran for President of the United States as an Independent. The democractic countries of the world have good cause to be thankful that Roosevelt won the election, although I wonder if FDR would have been quite so successful if his campaign funds had been as restricted as those of Ed Miles—who spent $76·33. Undeterred by yet another failure, Ed returned to Memphis and published a limited edition of 200 copies of a 170 page paperback book—so limited in fact that only one copy was completed. Needless to say, it was written, typeset, printed and bound by this lonely idealist, with an apology for his poor spelling and grammar. If that one copy was auctioned tomorrow, I suppose it could quite easily make enough to swell the funds of his Brotherhood to the amount he possessed before he started to build *Sturdy*. The pathos of this unhappy thought should (but won't) act as a deterrent to all other small boat idealists.

By the time Ed Miles arrived back in New York, Harry Pidgeon was off on his second world voyage, so Ed was the fourth and Harry the fifth (as well as being the second) single-handed circumnavigator. The sixth, a retired Captain in the French Merchant Service, Louis Bernicot, has often been misrepresented as an imitator of Slocum, because to this day he is the only other solo yachtsman to sail round the world via the Magellan Straits. In fact, Bernicot knew only about the exploits of Alain Gerbault when he decided to take the Straits route, and it was just by chance that he happened to read about Slocum in a magazine after he had made his decision. Equally, I have seen reports suggesting that he was a 'true hermit afloat'; these are not confirmed in Edward Allcard's introduction to Bernicot's book *The Voyage of the Anahita*, in which he states that the Captain told him in a letter that he sailed alone because 'nobody in his family cared to join him in the venture'.

Jean Louis Bernicot was nearly fifty-three when he sailed on August 22, 1936 in the 41 ft Bermudan cutter which he had had built for the voyage. He went back to sea for almost precisely the

111

same reason as Slocum, because his wife wanted him to run the family vineyard at Dordogne.* Bernicot had learned to come to terms with solitude, and like Slocum, could not afterwards bear to be parted from his beloved ship. He continued to sail *Anahita* after World War II until, in 1952, as so many wives have done with such husbands, she rebelled. She lashed out just once with a broken wire shroud; six weeks later the Captain died in France of a brain tumour as a result of this accidental blow on his head.

Bernicot's circumnavigation was one of the 'quiet' ones: unpublicized, unrewarded and unspectacular. It was, as one would expect of a man of the sea, merely an efficient twenty-one month cruise around the world. For this reason, if for no other, it should be better remembered than it is. Alas, it seems that nobody is interested in such dull voyages.

And so, from the first six named singlehanded round-the-worlders, plus Voss, we have very nearly covered the gamut of route and record possibilities: first westabout, first eastabout, first stunt, first partly crewed (for Voss sometimes had to sail alone for a time after the loss overboard of his second crewman), first double rounding, first using the Panama Canal, first using both Suez and Panama Canals, first using two vessels, first with auxiliary engine (both petrol and diesel), first Bermudan rig, first two-masted schooner, first three-masted schooner (Voss' *Tilikum*), first cutter, first yawl, first non-American (after the all-American 'firsts'), first troublefree . . . etc, etc.

All that is left, really, is the ultimate test of small boat seaworthiness: a solo voyage around the world in the Roaring Forties and the Screaming Fifties. Whether it was by coincidence or design the very next singlehander, the seventh, Vito Dumas from Argentina, accomplished this when he sailed *Lehg II* eastabout along the high latitude route in 1942–3. I will deal with his adventures with those of the other Cape Horners in the next chapter.

Of the rest, there is very little I can say here. It would take

*Nearly four years after his voyage, in 1902, Slocum purchased a small farm at West Tisbury, about in the centre of Martha's Vineyard (which is an island belonging to the state of Massachusetts, and not a vineyard) mainly because his wife Hettie had demanded a home she could call her own. Josh paid $305 for the property, later buying a woodland for $200. In spite of Hettie's dreams that she would be able to persuade the Captain to settle down, she was unsuccessful. The experiment collapsed in 1905, when Hettie began to take paying guests and Slocum went back to living on board *Spray*; later that year he cruised alone to the West Indies.

another book—and a thick one—to contain the variety of adventures experienced by all the singlehanded circumnavigators. It would be an impossible task, too, for although some have written about their voyages, others have quietly disappeared from the public eye without leaving a trace.

For example, the Israeli, Joseph Havkins, is very much a mystery man. I know that his intention was to sail round the world in the smallest boat, but his 23 ft yawl was bigger than John Guzzwell's 20 ft 6 in *Trekka* (which holds the 'smallest' record) and I am not even sure *when* he started, for Humphrey Barton in *Atlantic Adventurers* states that he crossed the Atlantic in 1953 and arrived in Australia in 1956, whereas according to my records, the years were 1956 and 1958 respectively. At all events, he did not use the Panama Canal; instead, he had his boat taken by road across Mexico.

John Guzzwell was the first Englishman to go round (another troublefree circumnavigation), but New Zealander Adrian Hayter was the first to start to go round under the British flag, although his two voyages, both commencing from England, cannot really be considered as a continuous round-the-world attempt. However, between 1950 and 1963 he undoubtedly completed a singlehanded circumnavigation. It can be seen that as we progress towards more recent events complications began to arise.

Bill Nance, whom I helped when he came to England from diamond mining in Africa, was the first solo yachtsman to circumnavigate eastabout via the three capes—Cape of Good Hope, Cape Leeuwin and Cape Horn—from and returning to the Northern Hemisphere: a total distance of 31,000 miles. I make this point now, as I did when Francis Chichester claimed to have made 'the first true circumnavigation by a singlehanded yacht rounding the three Capes: Horn, Leeuwin and Good Hope', because Chichester was *not* the first. Nance's achievement is discussed in greater detail in the following chapter.

Until Chichester was knighted by the Queen immediately after his voyage around the world, sponsorship was virtually unknown in this particular aspect of yachting. The early transatlantic voyagers and racers may have had plenty of backers, but not the circumnavigators. The French government had looked after Gerbault, and John Voss may have sailed with reward in mind, but by and large those who set forth to sail round the world alone could honestly claim that they had done so on their own resources. Chichester, however, had been supported by industrial backers, and privately by a distant relation, to the tune of £30,000, and from the completion of his voyage such sponsorship began to become fashionable. The Golden Globe Race non-stop round-the-world, promoted by the *Sunday Times* in 1968, was the next step in this direction, and Chay Blyth's non-stop circumnavigation westabout in the high latitudes was an inevitable sponsored extension of the idea. Ad-men put pens to paper and rejoiced at the change of dimension: John Masefield's *Sea Fever* was quoted and re-quoted with gusto, and Kenneth Grahame's 'messing about in boats' speech by Ratty became once again a philosophy for many landlubbers. The product was a surge of getting-away-from-it-all idealists, who seldom escaped from anything—including debts, and their responsibilities.

So when Francis Chichester was knighted, a great deal of speculation about small boat record breaking crashed upon the public like a mighty *tsunami*. A fair proportion of the statements made were either misleading or completely inaccurate.

To set the records straight, *Gipsy Moth IV* was then the largest yacht to be sailed round singlehanded (currently she is the fourth largest in length overall); Chichester was the first man to go round the world alone with only one stopover (to date, five single-handers have gone round without any stops); his passage times, port to port, were the fastest then, although it must be pointed out that there was no opposition except Bill Nance's tiny $4\frac{1}{2}$ ton *Vertue* (which nevertheless on one occasion in the South Atlantic achieved an amazing 192 miles in twenty-five hours). Chichester was not the oldest person to complete a solo circum-navigation (he was sixty-six, whereas Pidgeon was sixty-eight at the completion of his second voyage); nor, as I have mentioned, was he the first to sail this route, although I am sure he genuinely believed that he was. So his only record which still stands is that he was the first to circumnavigate alone with only one stopover. These facts should not in any way detract from Chichester's very obvious and magnificent 'first'.

Equally, the claim that Robin Knox-Johnston was 'the first man to sail around the world non-stop, singlehanded', is *not* correct. Without quibbling, the first to circumnavigate non-stop and singlehanded was the Frenchman, Bernard Moitessier, in his 39 ft 6 in steel Bermudan ketch *Joshua*. He 'tied the knot' early in March 1969, by crossing his outward track, which had started from Plymouth on August 22 the year before; he took some 145 days to circle the globe back to this spot, which was approximately

700 miles west of Cape Town. He then continued on across the Indian Ocean a second time, and to Tahiti (Papeete) in the Pacific. The third singlehander to circumnavigate non-stop was the South African Nigel Tetley, in his 40 ft trimaran *Victress*: he left Plymouth on September 16, 1968 and tied the knot on April 22, 1969 after 179 days. However, Knox-Johnston's homeward track did not cross his outward track until he was very nearly back at his starting port of Falmouth, where he arrived at 1525 on—yet another coincidence—April 22, 1969: the same day as Tetley tied his knot, and only two hours, thirty-five minutes before him. (I am assuming that Knox-Johnston did not cross his outward track until he crossed the finishing line, although this seems unlikely.) So Bernard Moitessier was the first man to achieve a non-stop, singlehanded circumnavigation, with Robin Knox-Johnston second, nearly six weeks later, and Nigel Tetley a close, almost simultaneous, third.

By pointing out those errors in popular claims, I am not attempting to deride the achievements of those singlehanders. Until I began to look closely into such records, I did not know for certain who, really, had done what. My main grumble is that nobody else really bothered to find out, and I blame the promoters, the sponsors and the Establishment for failing to notice these rather obvious blind spots. The sponsors, I suppose, couldn't have cared less, but surely there is some yachting organization which could have been more actively involved in sorting out the details.

Of course, Britain can claim that Knox-Johnston was the first singlehander to complete a 'long' non-stop voyage around the world, from and back to the Northern Hemisphere, but it doesn't sound quite the same thing.

Similarly, Chay Blyth's lonely non-stop battle westabout around Cape Horn, almost entirely in the high latitudes, was undoubtedly a 'first', and an incredible effort. Yet little credit was given to Marcel Bardiaux, who was actually the first person to circumnavigate in this direction via Cape Horn and the Cape of Good Hope—even although he did not complete this section of the voyage entirely in the Roaring Forties (wisely he went north, into the warmth of the central Pacific). Bardiaux also retains another record: 543 landfalls in the seven-plus years which he took to get round; and nobody will deny the dangers implied by this multiple proximity of land, which is generally *avoided* as much as possible by most blue-water yachtsmen.

115

Finally, coming right up to date, there is the remarkable record made by Alain Colas in the 70 ft aluminium trimaran *Manureva* (ex *Pen Duick IV*), who circumnavigated solo from St Malo, France via Sydney back to St Malo, eastabout, in 167 days (1973–4)—fifty-nine days faster than Chichester's time over this route. During the same period Chay Blyth, with a crew of paratroopers varying in number from nine to twelve, sailed the 72 ft ketch *Great Britain II* in the Whitbread/RNSA Round the World Race (Portsmouth–Cape Town–Sydney–Rio de Janeiro–Portsmouth) in 144 days, thus equalling the very fast times set up by two of Donald McKay's clipper ships, *Marco Polo* and *Lightning*, in 1852 and 1854 respectively, but not beating the world's record circumnavigation under sail set by another McKay ship, the American built, British owned *James Baines*, which completed the voyage Liverpool–Melbourne–Liverpool in 132 days during 1854–5 (sixty-three days' outward passage; sixty-nine days home). The record for a British built ship, the iron-hulled *Patriarch*, was sixty-nine days from London to Sydney, and sixty-nine days from Sydney to London (138 days total) in 1869.

It should be noted that the Melbourne passage is some 2000 miles shorter than that to Sydney, using the most direct routes: approximately 23,500 miles against 25,500 miles. For purposes of comparison, when working out average speeds for these record circumnavigations I allowed 27,000 miles for the total distance via Melbourne, and 29,000 miles via Sydney—although it must also be recognized that *Great Britain II* called at two additional ports. However, even with these arbitrary mileages the results are interesting:

(1) *Patriarch*   8·8 knots average speed
(2) *James Baines*   8·5 knots average speed
(3) *Great Britain II*   8·4 knots average speed
(4) *Manureva* (solo)   7·2 knots average speed
(5) *Gipsy Moth IV* (solo) 5·5 knots average speed

So the position now is that a singlehanded trimaran is only thirty-five days behind the world's record total time for a 'long' circumnavigation under sail, but it seems extremely unlikely that a singlehanded monohull will ever again catch up on the rapidly widening gap of eighty-two days between Chichester's time and the fastest ever yacht record of 144 days.

Well, you will find them all listed in Appendix 2, and a more varied and assorted crowd of individual adventurers would be impossible to imagine. Most, if not all, can claim either a 'first' or a record of one sort or another. I have done my best, but I'm afraid I was unable to find out everything about everybody. It is more than likely that I have even missed out some names, and I can only hope that somebody, some time, will help me to make this list more accurate and detailed than it is now.

8
The Cape Horners

Taking *Charter Oak* in 1857 as the first recorded two-crew boat, and *Centennial* in 1876 as the first proven singlehanded yacht to make transatlantic crossings, it is interesting to note that from these dates, only in sailing around the world and transatlantic racing have the loners shown the way to the vessels crewed by two or more.

Actually, the first two-man circumnavigation was made by the American William Albert Robinson, accompanied for most of the voyage by the Tahitian Etera: they sailed westabout via Panama and Suez in the 32 ft Bermudan ketch *Svaap*, during the years 1928–31, thirty years or so after Slocum. The first transatlantic race in *small* yachts with normal crews did not take place until as recently as 1950, when *Cohoe* (32 ft 1 in), *Samuel Pepys* (30 ft 1 in), *Makoia* (39 ft 3 in), *Karin III* (41 ft 6 in), *Gulvain* (55 ft) raced from Bermuda to Plymouth, Devon: *Gulvain* sailed the 3000-odd miles in eighteen days, three hours, but *Cohoe* won in a corrected time of fourteen days, seven hours, twenty-one minutes, although her actual time was also very good for such a small vessel, loaded with a total crew of four: twenty-one days, nine hours, fourteen minutes.

But when we investigate the small boat Cape Horners, we find that a two-manned yacht was easily the first to beat this terrible natural barrier which so nearly divides the Atlantic from the Pacific.

Before the opening of the Panama Canal on August 15, 1914 all sailing ships voyaging between these two oceans were forced to

118

use the Cape Horn route. Willem Schouten had first christened the place when he rounded it in 1616, but I do not know who was responsible for naming the dreadful winds which howl almost continuously over those bleak seas.

The Roaring Forties and the Screaming Fifties! Across the South Atlantic and past the Cape of Good Hope they thunder into the vastness of the Southern Indian Ocean. With 5000 miles to the nearest land, Australia—not counting the tiny Prince Edward, St Paul and Amsterdam Islands, the lonely Crozets or bleak Kerguelen—this was the area where, over a century ago, so many of the beautiful clipper ships broke record after record on the Australian run. Past Tasmania, past New Zealand, the gales and wild seas press eastwards across another 6000 miles of utter isolation: not an island nor even a rock disturbs their progress there. And then at last, having raced untrammelled for so many thousands of miles, the storms approach the one and only barrier in the whole of their journey around the world. Funnelled savagely into the narrow gap called Drake Strait, with the tiny island of Cape Horn and the rocky shores of Tierra del Fuego to the north and bleak Graham Land to the south, (plus a great deal of ice, depending on the time of the year), the accumulated strength of wind and sea reaches a crescendo of power. Here lies the end of the world: a seaman's nightmare if ever there was one.

The yawl *Pandora*, built to the same lines as Slocum's *Spray*, sailed from Bunbury in Western Australia on May 3, 1910, skippered by her English owner George Blythe, with a Greek-Australian crew Peter Arapakis. Their intention was to sail round the world via Cape Horn and the Cape of Good Hope. Their final point of departure was Sydney, which they left on July 10.

They were pooped, and suffered a knockdown in the tempestuous Tasman Sea, and had to spend a month in New Zealand repairing the damage. Then they set off again on October 2 across the Pacific, via Pitcairn and Easter Island. On January 16, 1911 they rounded Cape Horn, three and a half miles off their port beam, in a gale. Six days later they were under bare poles near the Falklands, when *Pandora* was capsized by a gigantic wave. Fortunately the men were below at the time. Both masts broke off when the yawl was inverted, and then another wave rolled her upright. The two men fought on the sea-swept decks to clear the tangled masts and rigging before they pounded a hole in the hull. They managed to cut them away after a desperate struggle, afterwards using the clutter of wreckage as a sea anchor. They were lucky enough to be found the next day by a Norwegian whaling ship, which towed them some ten miles to their whale station at New Island in the West Falklands. Here *Pandora* was repaired once again.

She left on March 4, 1911 for St Helena and Ascension Islands; from here they sailed 4850 miles direct to New York in forty-six days. The well known self-steering capabilities of *Spray* were proved throughout this voyage, but particularly on the last leg when the only duties of the helmsman were to check the course of *Pandora* once every twenty-four hours at noon.*

In spite of the two setbacks, *Pandora* had covered 22,000 miles at an average sailing speed of 120 m.p.d., or just under five knots. Contrary to the opinion of many experienced yachtsmen over the years, *Spray* and the several copies of her were *not* slow ships, even if the apple bows and barn-door transom tended to make them look so. As to stability, it seems that the cunning skill of old Josh Slocum was an essential ingredient for survival—although the Strouts managed well enough in *Igdrasil.*

Blythe and Arapakis departed from New York on July 30 for London. They were never seen again. Although the Roaring Forties and evil Cape Horn had done their damnedest, *Pandora* and her unfortunate crew were finally beaten by the north Atlantic—a fact which is not generally known.

After *Pandora*, the first small yacht to round Cape Horn was the Irish ketch *Saoirse* (42' × 12' × 6'9"), owned and skippered by Conor O'Brien. She sailed around the world eastabout, via the three Capes, during the years 1923–5. The crew varied in number from port to port, but totalled four during the forty-six day run from Auckland, New Zealand to the Falklands. O'Brien published an account of this voyage in *Across Three Oceans* (Allan, 1927).

---

*Even this amazing demonstration by *Pandora* is nothing when compared with the original. Of his voyage from Thursday Island to the Cocos-Keeling group in the Indian Ocean, a distance of 2700 miles covered at an average of just over 117 m.p.d., Slocum wrote: 'I didn't touch the helm, for with the current and heave of the sea the sloop found herself at the end of the run absolutely in the fairway of the channel. Then at last I trimmed the sails, took the helm, and flogged her up the couple of miles or so abreast the harbour landing where I cast anchor at 3.30 p.m., July 17, 1897, twenty-three days from Thursday Island. During those twenty-three days I had not spent altogether more than three hours at the helm, including the time occupied in beating into Keeling harbour. I just lashed the helm and let her go; whether the wind was abeam or dead aft, it was all the same: she always sailed on her course.'

The very first singlehander to double the Cape did it the hard way: from east to west, against the prevailing winds and sea.

Alfon Möller Hansen, a Norwegian from Forvik, was a seaman by trade from a very early age, but only with the object of saving money to buy his own boat, as he was determined 'to make the ocean and small craft voyaging my career'. In due course he purchased a Colin Archer double-ender; a *redningskjoite* or lifeboat of the Norwegian Coast Patrol, which he named *Mary Jane*. This heavily built and sparred 36 ft gaff-rigged sloop, built of 2 in oak planking on 7 × 6 in pine frames, had only an Armstrong auxiliary—a long sweep or oar. For crew, Al carried Mate, a black dog, and Sailor, a grey cat. He left Oslo on July 15, 1932.

He called at Weymouth in Dorset (where he earned some money fitting out the yacht *New Moss Rose* for a local publican), Gijon, Oporto and Lisbon (where he had to sell his sea boots to raise some cash for provisions). Then on to Las Palmas, leaving on November 12, 1932 to cross the Atlantic to Miami, taking forty-three days, with a best day's run of 176 miles.

We have already seen how Howard Blackburn and Ann Davison came down the Mississippi; Al Hansen, for some incredible reason, decided, and managed, to navigate *up* this river; he then crossed the Great Lakes, to arrive back in the Atlantic via the St Lawrence. Some journey in a motorless sailing vessel! He then cruised leisurely southwards to Buenos Aires. 'It is best not to make definite plans,' he once remarked. 'Fate may sometimes force one to abandon them, or deviate. My voyaging is not made in search of anything but contentment...'

Very little is known about Al's rounding of Cape Horn in 1934. He sailed from Buenos Aires, and arrived at Ancud at the northern tip of the Isle of Chiloe 110 days later. They must have been very terrible days, as his average speed of only 30 m.p.d. indicates. After a brief rest, he set off again for ports up the western seaboard of South America and disappeared. Some months later wreckage from the *Mary Jane* was found on the southern coast of Chile, and thus it was proved that Alfon Hansen had made his last departure. Nevertheless he has left his mark, as he was the first singlehander to round Cape Horn, and the first to do so westabout—the hard way.

Nine years later the Argentine rancher and farmer Vito Dumas became the first singlehander to round the Cape eastabout—and live to write a book about his experiences. He left Buenos Aires on June 27, 1942 and returned on September 7, 1943 having

121

covered 20,420 miles of the stormiest waters in the world in 272 sailing days. He had called at only three ports: Cape Town, Wellington in New Zealand, and Valparaiso, Chile; and had sailed south of four Capes, not three. All in the tiny (31′2″ × 10′9″ × 5′8″) ketch *Lehg II*.

Next to go round was the Frenchman Marcel Bardiaux, who spent six years (a total working time of 15,000 hours) building his 30′8″ × 8′10″ × 5′9″ Bermudan sloop *Les Quatre Vents* (*Les 4 Vents* on her transom) in which he subsequently completed a circumnavigation westabout via the two Capes, the Horn and Good Hope, taking nearly eight years. He rounded the Horn on May 12, 1952.

He was followed by Bill Watson, who from December 13, 1962 to September 12, 1963 not only thoroughly explored the coastline to the *west* (the weather side) of Tierra del Fuego in his self-built 34 ft cutter *Freedom*, but actually had a swim in the icy water at the very base of the 1391 ft pinnacle which marks the southernmost tip of the South American continent. After a leisurely cruise in these waters, Watson sold *Freedom* in Punta Arenas. 'She had served me well, but considering that she had cost me only about $900 to build, including the new Mercedes engine, and that I got more than double this for her, I let her go and replaced her with a more modern boat.' He had built her on a mud bank in the Valdivia River in Chile.

He was followed by the Australian Bill Nance, in *Cardinal Vertue*. This 25′3″ × 7′2″ × 4′6″ Bermudan sloop is to date the smallest yacht to circumnavigate via the three Capes, and was at the time the smallest to double Cape Horn, which she did on January 7, 1965, thirty-eight days out of Auckland, New Zealand. However, this record has now been beaten by the Japanese yachtsman Hiroshi Aoki (Appendix 4).

Next came an Old Etonian, Englishman Edward Allcard, aged fifty-three, in his Bermudan ketch *Sea Wanderer* (36′ × 11′ × 5′4″). She had been built shortly after the turn of the century, and her sixty-four year old frames and planking were not up to the very bad weather which Allcard had to face. With his yacht leaking badly throughout the battle against gales and heavy seas during April 1966, being forced back into the Atlantic on several occasions by the vicious conditions, Allcard and *Sea Wanderer* finally made it into the Pacific on the 12th, and sailed on towards Valparaiso to continue their slowest ever solo circumnavigation.

Almost a year after Allcard passed the longitude of Cape Horn, Francis Chichester rounded eastabout, which put him into seventh place in the steadily lengthening list of singlehanded Cape Horners. *Gipsy Moth IV* was watched on television by millions as she wallowed through heavy seas off the Cape on March 20, 1967.

It would be nice to leave the matter tidily at this point, but unfortunately small boat records are seldom an easy matter to resolve. In the first place, Bill Watson did not actually *sail* south of Cape Horn; in the second place, there is the matter of 'the three Capes'. Although Watson approached Cape Horn from the direction of Diego Ramirez Island, he altered course to pass *north* of Horn Island (the southern tip of which is called Cape Horn). He then anchored *Freedom* in Foam Cove, on the northeast corner of this small island, and later moved her to the southeast anchorage under the lee, and only about a mile from the peak which we know as Cape Horn. From here he paddled a small folding canoe right round the Cape and then back to *Freedom*, and it was during this trip that he had a swim. So Bill Watson's *double* rounding in his canoe will no doubt be quibbled at by many.

The distinction of 'the three Capes' is somewhat easier to resolve. Cape Horn, as already explained, is really a rocky hill on a small island, roughly 200 miles from the southernmost tip of the mainland of South America, Cape Froward. Equally, the Cape of Good Hope is *not* the southernmost point of the African continent as is generally supposed: it is beaten by Cape Agulhas which lies about eighty miles to the east of Good Hope, and extends some thirty miles further south. However, as most people know about the former, and hardly anybody knows about the latter, by common consent the Cape of Good Hope is popularly regarded as the southern tip of Africa. Similarly Cape Leeuwin on the southwest corner of Western Australia is neither the westernmost nor the southernmost point in this area. It was, however, the most easily sighted landfall for sailing ships running their easting down across the Southern Indian Ocean. These are the three Capes referred to by Chichester and others.

While sorting out the Roaring Forties records for this book, however, it became evident to me that the three Capes were insufficient for analysing voyages subsequent to Chichester. The best distinction seemed to be *five* Capes, because only when all five were rounded could any vessel claim to have sailed entirely round the world in the Roaring Forties. The additional two Capes are South East Cape, at the extreme southern end of the island of

123

Tasmania, and South West Cape, the southernmost point of Stewart Island, which is separated from South Island, New Zealand by the wide Foveaux Strait.

Vito Dumas had rounded the three Capes and also South East Cape in Tasmania. Sir Francis Chichester, in a letter to me after he had completed his circumnavigation, called this a 'small circumnavigation', and added that Bill Nance's voyage came into the same category. 'I feel that a *true circumnavigation* should pass through two points on the earth's surface antipodean to each other', he wrote. I quite agree. But with these types of records it is not as simple as that.

'Two points antipodean to each other' means one point on the globe diametrically opposite another. A convenient, round-figure position near Chichester's port of departure, Plymouth, is Lat. 50°N, Long. 5°W and the point antipodean to this lies some hundreds of miles to the south of South Island, New Zealand. But Chichester actually sailed *north* of North Island—more than 1000 miles from a 'true' circumnavigation through two points antipodean to each other, if the start line is taken as one of them.

Chichester rounded only the three Capes, and Bill Nance did the same. Nance sailed from England in September 1962, calling at Buenos Aires, Cape Town, Fremantle, Melbourne, Auckland— and back to Buenos Aires to tie the knot. Chichester tied his knot some distance out in the South Atlantic and slightly north of the Buenos Aires parallel (he tied it a second time on the Equator). From there, Nance made a fast passage to the West Indies, Nassau and on to Florida, sailing a total distance of just on 31,000 miles around the world. Chichester's mileage was slightly less: just under 30,000.

In my opinion, therefore, the Australian Bill Nance was the first singlehander to complete a solo 'long' circumnavigation from and back to the Northern Hemisphere, via the three Capes, eastabout.

Francis Chichester was the first to complete a long circumnavigation with only one stopover.

Vito Dumas was the first singlehander to sail a 'small' or 'short' circumnavigation south of four Capes (including South East Cape, Tasmania).

Alex Rose very nearly completed a 'true' circumnavigation through two antipodean points with only one stopover, sailing south of four Capes (including South East Cape, Tasmania), but he can only be credited with a 'long'.

124

Robin Knox-Johnston was the first to complete a non-stop 'long' circumnavigation south of the three Capes.

Bernard Moitessier, however, soon broke these simple rules. He sailed a total distance of 37,455 miles when he decided against continuing his competition in the Golden Globe Race of 1968–9.

After rounding Cape Horn on February 5, 1969 Moitessier approached the Falklands. '. . . already tired by the nervous tension involved in rounding the Horn, I could hardly stand when *Joshua* hove into view of Port Stanley lighthouse at the mouth of the fjord, February 9, four days later.' He tried to attract attention by signalling with a mirror, but it was a Sunday and the lighthouse seemed empty. Yet he wanted to pass a message to his family that he was all right. He hove-to. Nobody saw him. He sat in the cockpit staring towards infinity and absorbing the gentle rhythm of the sea under his hove-to vessel. Soon his mind was as relaxed as *Joshua*'s motion: thinking and decision making could wait: he set course northeast, to keep clear of possible ice, and returned to his bunk. Days later, when the dangers of ice lay to the south, he swam in a wetsuit and scraped barnacles from *Joshua*'s bottom. Here was peace; there, back in Europe, was (as he called it) the snakepit. Finally, after much soul-searching, Moitessier chose peace. He set *Joshua* on course for Tahiti, just as Fletcher Christian had done directly after he had deposed Captain Bligh almost exactly 180 years before. The call of the islands: the last hope of escape. And in so doing, he posed an additional record problem, for altogether he sailed non-stop south of all five Capes, and then round four of them for a second time: Good Hope, Leeuwin, South East, South West, Horn, Good Hope, Leeuwin, South East, South West—and finally northwards to Tahiti. Approximately one and a half times round the world—and yet he did not re-pass over two points antipodean to each other, nor did he return to the Northern Hemisphere to qualify for a 'long' circumnavigation (even although his was the longest non-stop voyage ever).

Technically, the first solo yachtsman to sail through a position antipodean (actually he went further south) on the earth's surface to his starting and finishing line in the Northern Hemishpere was the Japanese circumnavigator Kenichi Horie in his 28 ft 10 in sloop *Mermaid III* (1973–4). (See Appendices 2 and 4.)

It can now be seen clearly that it is an impossible job to sort out fairly these small boat 'firsts'.

Speeds, too, are no simple matter.

Unless *every* skipper specifically records his fastest noon-to-noon, or one week, or between-two-points, or between-two-longitudes, (etc) speed averages or distance run, it is generally impossible to verify somebody else's claim. For example, Sir Francis Chichester wrote to me suggesting the following record: 'In 1966 I made a straight-line passage of 4000 miles in thirty-one days, six and a half hours at the average speed of 127·8 miles per day. The distance sailed was 4427 miles. I believe that was the fastest singlehanded passage at that time.'

Well, Sir Francis started the ball rolling, but to check all the possible 4000 mile passages made by singlehanders would be quite impracticable unless one could gain access to all the relevant logbooks, which itself would become a full time job as more and more claims were made. And as we have seen, if *Pandora* could cover 22,000 miles at an average speed of 120 m.p.d., there is every likelihood that a less tubby yacht, sailed singlehanded, may have beaten Chichester's 127.8 m.p.d. I just don't know.

Similarly, a great deal of controversy has been aroused in the past, and to the present day, by the speed records of square-rigged clipper ships. Certainly some of the noon-to-noon distance figures must remain suspect. Here, for example, is an extract from the shipboard news sheet *Champion of the Seas Gazette*, printed during her maiden voyage from Liverpool to Melbourne.

CAPTAIN'S REPORT—DECEMBER 15, 1854

Ladies and Gentlemen,
   I again submit to you our weekly report which shows a very fair distance. Unfortunately in the early part of the week we had a heavy gale from the NW which compelled us to run the ship somewhat to leeward of our course, yet the distance made that day by *Champion of the Seas* is without a parallel. Should we be favoured with any ordinary luck, another week will terminate our passage.

Dec. 9th	Lat. 46°49'S	Long. 75°08'E	222 miles
Dec. 10th	Lat. 46°44'S	Long. 81°55'E	297 miles
Dec. 11th	Lat. 47°01'S	Long. 88°31'E	289 miles
Dec. 12th	Lat. 49°58'S	Long. 99°15'E	465 miles
Dec. 13th	No observations		
Dec. 14th	Lat. 45°42'S	Long. 104°46'E	341 miles
Dec. 15th	Lat. 43°08'S	Long. 109°30'E	215 miles

Total in nautical miles: 1829

Disbelievers have gleefully pointed out that on the day after the record-breaking run the sun was conveniently hidden from view, so that only dead reckoning navigation was possible: 'There's many a crook 'twixt the log and the book.' They also point out that the week's run only averages out at 261 m.p.d., and that the average run for the whole passage was 199 m.p.d. Well, that's true enough, but I'd still rather believe men of action than all the armchair theorists at home who decry such claims.

For example, Chichester claimed another record-breaking run of 1017¾ miles in five days during a later passage in *Gipsy Moth V* : averaging 203 m.p.d. I did not question his accuracy—even to the three-quarters of a mile, which seemed to be impossibly precise— but I am not in a position to state categorically that this was the fastest ever run over five days made by a singlehander, and to this day I still do not know.

To pick a 'fastest' noon-to-noon, five day or seven day run from a long passage is certainly not unreasonable from the point of view of the singlehander or the captain of a clipper, but it presents an almost impossible situation for a collator of facts— such as myself—who cannot, even with the best lists ever compiled of singlehanded voyages, compare such a record with many—if any!—others, since few singlehanders seem to bother about such matters.

Over long distances, however, a more reasonable understanding of this type of record is possible. For example, the fastest speeds attained by clippers in the Roaring Forties, which even the most critical theorists do not seem to have contested, are as follows.

During March 1853 the Donald McKay clipper *Sovereign of the Seas* on passage from Honolulu to New York ran before a northwesterly gale for twelve days, covering 3736 nautical miles at an average speed of 311 m.p.d.; her fastest noon-to-noon run was on March 18, in Lat. 52°12′S, Long. 91°28′W, when she covered 411 miles.

The fastest Australia to Cape Horn passage was made by the Donald McKay clipper *Lightning*. She left Melbourne on August 20, 1854 and rounded Cape Horn one hour over nineteen days later, averaging about 340 m.p.d. (my approximation since I do not know the precise distance sailed). In the first ten days of this incredible run she covered 3722 miles at an average speed of 372 m.p.d., on her best day achieving 421 miles.

The fastest comparable singlehanded passage was made by Krzysztof Baranowski, a Pole, when he departed from Hobart, Tasmania on January 10, 1973 and rounded Cape Horn on

February 23, taking forty-five days for the slightly shorter course. (The sea distance from Melbourne to Hobart is 443 miles, but the clipper *Lightning* probably shortened this by going through Bass Strait, on a direct route towards Stewart Island.)

The only comparable passages by singlehanded Cape Horners (i.e. from, or near, Hobart) were as follows:

Bill King: Fremantle to the Horn. At noon on December 23, 1972 King was 180 miles due south of Hobart. From this longitude to the Horn he took forty-five days—the same time as Baranowski, but over a somewhat shorter course.

Bernard Moitessier: Hobart to the Horn, December 18 to February 5, 1969: forty-nine days.

The other Cape Horners who sailed direct from either Australia or New Zealand to the Horn recorded the following times:

Bill Nance: from Auckland, North Island, New Zealand, in thirty-eight days.

Francis Chichester: from Sydney, going north of New Zealand, in fifty days.

Alec Rose: from Bluff, south of South Island, New Zealand in fifty-five days.

Robin Knox-Johnston: from Otago, south of South Island, New Zealand in fifty-seven days.

Nigel Tetley: also from Otago, in 44 days.

Alain Colas, who had already beaten the cream of solo racing monohulls in the 1972 OSTAR (including the mighty 128'0 × 18'5" × 11'3" schooner, *Vendredi 13*) with his trimaran *Pen Duick IV*, sailed from St Malo, France to Sydney, Australia in the very fast time of seventy-nine days (twenty-eight days faster than Chichester's time). He left Sydney on December 29, 1973 and rounded the Horn on February 4, 1974 (where he was supplied with some petrol for his generator by the Royal Navy ship *Endurance*). This thirty-seven day passage in the six year old trimaran, originally designed by André Allegré as Eric Tabarly's entry in the 1968 OSTAR and re-named *Manureva* after winning the 1972 OSTAR, will undoubtedly be the most difficult to beat of all the many speed records mentioned.

In the reverse direction, Chay Blyth took sixty-one days from Cape Horn to clear Foveaux Strait which, as I have already

128

mentioned, divides South Island of New Zealand from Stewart Island.

So there you have all the singlehanded, high latitude records across the South Pacific. Without elaborate measurements of every track, in my opinion Bill Nance's time from Auckland to the Horn—thirty-eight days—in his tiny *Cardinal Vertue* is easily the best passage of them all when size-for-size the contesting monohulls are taken into consideration; of the amazing *Manureva* I have the greatest admiration—but she is obviously in a class of her own.

And while on the subject of size I should mention the remarkable Japanese singlehander Yoh Aoki, who sailed the tiny 20 ft yawl *Ahodori*, which he had built himself of ply, from Osaka to San Francisco in 1971, and from there to Buenos Aires via Mazatlan, Acapulco, Galapagos, Easter Island and Cape Horn, which he rounded on January 12, 1973. *Ahodori* means *Crazy Bird* in Japanese; this, surely, is a most suitable name for the smallest yacht ever to *sail* round Cape Horn (not forgetting Bill Watson paddling around in his canoe).

I started this chapter with a horrific picture of the Cape Horn region. But from my brief descriptions it would appear that most of the singlehanders rounded the dreadful place without too much bother. Well, most of them did, and some of the stories which you may have heard were probably connected with crewed yachts.

Al Hansen undoubtedly had a long and weary struggle to get round, but I do not know the details. Vito Dumas was below, repairing an instrument by the light of a paraffin lamp, when, just after midnight, he was flung across the cabin so violently that his face crashed against a deadlight and he was knocked out for several minutes. This happened during a violent squall from the north. He had broken his nose and injured his mouth so badly that it bled for some days afterwards whenever he tried to eat. 'Cape Horn', Dumas remarked in his book, 'had made me pay toll.'

In contrast, Bill Watson paddled about the dreaded place as though it was a coral beach in some sheltered lagoon. And Nigel Tetley had some difficulty getting round because he was becalmed; this he regarded as fortuitous since it was suppertime, and he cooked and ate an excellent meal, and toasted Cape Horn with a bottle of wine, while waiting for a wind.

Of all the singlehanded Cape Horners, Marcel Bardiaux undoubtedly suffered the most. Here is a piece of blood-and-thunder which I wrote many years ago for a children's annual, and which seems appropriate to conclude this chapter.

Specially designed by the French naval architect H Dervin, *Les 4 Vents* looks no different from the multitudes of small yachts which sail around our shores every summer. With a lead keel of 3000 lbs and a total displacement of 9000 lbs she is self-righting. She is unsinkable too, due partly to twenty-four buoyancy tanks bolted to the frame inside the hull, and partly to a large rubber raft spread below decks and readily inflated by compressed air in an emergency. The tiny cockpit is not self-draining—but the door of the cabin will close automatically if any water comes aboard.

These are just a few of the novel features which Bardiaux incorporated in his ship. From his special all-in-one water and wind proof survival suit, to his self-designed double ended 40 lbs collapsible lifeboat capable of holding five adults, Bardiaux did his best to be prepared—and it was just as well that he did.

As soon as he entered the treacherous Le Maire Strait, which separates Staten Island from Tierra del Fuego, Bardiaux and his tiny yacht felt the full weight of the biting winds and icy seas. Here in May, 1952 he prepared for his first battle against the timeless ferocity of the elements. Perhaps the very particles of air which tore through his rigging at 50 knots, forcing him to lower his mainsail and substitute a 60 sq ft storm sail, were part of the same gale which drove *Lightning* eastabout nearly 100 years before. Nature does not need to invent new methods of destruction when the old ones are so powerful.

The opposition was overwhelming. *Les 4 Vents* plunged and twisted, striving to work against the spume-streaked rollers. But they were too much for her. Bardiaux went below to assemble his sea anchor. As he disappeared into the cabin, clawing his way to the forepeak, clutching with frozen fingers for handholds to prevent himself from being hurled to leeward, a vicious gust slammed the yacht on its beam ends. For a brief moment she lay on her side. Bardiaux tried to get back to the cockpit to release the rigid mainsheet—to ease her somehow from the frightful pressure of wind . . .

He was too late. Freezing water burst through the open door, which slammed and locked. The ship lurched: over she went—upside down. Bardiaux, in total darkness, held on and prayed. A crash startled him: his heavy anchor had broken adrift. A thud followed—had the mast snapped?

Les 4 Vents sprang upright as the storm sail split under the water. The sudden snap-back, with the lead keel exerting full leverage, together with a final thrust from wind and sea, whirled her right over again so that she completed a second roll. She had suffered two capsizes in almost as many seconds.

Yet somehow, in spite of losing his first bout, Bardiaux went on to conquer. Although his yacht was sheathed in ice from the capsizing, he steered her into Aquirre Bay to pump her dry and get some rest. The next day he sailed westward to anchor on the lee of Deceit Island for the night, this time within sight of his objective. On May 12, 1952, with strong westerly winds still opposing him, he rounded Cape Horn.

So Marcel Bardiaux, his right leg paralysed from the intense cold, survived, and went on to sail alone around the world—the ninth man to accomplish this feat. But he was the first to do it westabout via Cape Horn.

This concludes the account of the singlehanded Cape Horners—or as much of the truth as I have been able to assemble to date. I am sure that there must be others who, like Hansen, Nance, Watson and Allcard (and possibly Harrison), received little or no publicity because they did not write books about their experiences. I simply cannot believe, for example, that a lone American hasn't been round—particularly in view of the early American participation in virtually every aspect of singlehanded transocean sailing.

But those are all the names that I can find to date: the men who have achieved the Mount Everest of small-boat endeavour.

The Cape Horners!

9
Other Record-breakers

It has proved an extraordinarily difficult task to collate even the major singlehanded voyages and records into some semblance of order. What is not generally realized, or appreciated, is how many hundreds of singlehanders—perhaps thousands—have sailed every conceivable route all over the world without recognition. It is therefore to some extent understandable that the subject has become so confused with inexactitudes.

The comparatively recent commercial interest in small boat records has not helped either. Sponsors, promotors, ad-men and the like have disrupted the gentle flow of casual adventuring with an avalanche of claims to add appeal to their current projects— almost always without making any attempt at all to find out who did what before their present hero or heroine. Spontaneous 'news' is the order of the day: to hell with difficult-to-obtain facts. In this respect, publishers' blurbs on the jackets of so many recent books should not be taken as truth. Indeed, it is doubtful if the superlatives clacked onto paper via a sub's typewriter are ever really intended as a definitive or lasting statement.

The trouble, however, is that the public accepts such claims as gospel, and in a very short space of time a Drake or Bligh type of legend is born. By revealing faults in the claims made by, or on behalf of, such famous people as Chichester, Knox-Johnston, Nicolette Milnes Walker, et al. I am not attempting to detract attention from their undoubtedly excellent voyages, merely trying to get the conglomeration of claims into some order. With singlehanded circumnavigators this has been difficult enough, even though many have written books, but with all the other records it is very nearly an impossible task to sort out the true facts—and be sure that the answers are the right ones.

Take multihulls for example. Having written two books about trimarans, and one about the philosophical problems which should be considered during the dreaming stage, before setting forth, one would think that I ought to know who has done what in these three-hulled craft, and something of what has been accomplished in catamarans too. Well, I do know a little, of course, but I'd soon be damned if I became too emphatic.

I can state with reasonable certainty that the first transocean voyage accomplished by a 'modern' multihull (it wasn't exactly modern, since it was copied from a Polynesian design of about a thousand years before), with Europeans for crew, was made by Eric de Bisschop and Joseph Tatiboet (both French), when they sailed the 38 ft catamaran *Kaimiloa* from Honolulu to Cannes via the Cape of Good Hope, in 264 days during 1937–8. Equally, the very first trimaran to cross two oceans with a crew of two was the 30 ft Piver-designed Nimble class *Trinui*, whose crew of two Englishmen, Alex Grimes and Roy Garsides, sailed from Wells in Norfolk to New Zealand during 1962–3. But these were two-crew voyages. Who were the first singlehanders?

Discounting the undoubtedly original multihull voyages made across the Pacific long before Brendan was exploring the Atlantic, some of which may have been accomplished by single-handers, I believe David Landgraf (USA) made the first solo voyage across an ocean in a trimaran when he sailed his Piver-designed Nugget class (24′ × 14′ × 1′6″) Bermudan sloop *Golden Fleece* from Ensenada, Mexico to Hawaii in 1963.

During 1964 two tris crossed the Atlantic singlehanded. The first, owned by L A 'Red' Stolle (USA), was a Piver-designed Victress class ketch (almost identical to Nigel Tetley's *Victress*, launched by the same yard, Contour Craft Ltd, the year before), which he named *Fancy Three*. She was purchased partially from funds supplied by radio 'hams' from America and all over the world who wanted to contact this new floating radio station. Stolle was himself a ham, and *Fancy Three* was the first multihull ham radio station as well as being (I think) the first singlehanded tri to cruise across the Atlantic.

The other tri which crossed the Atlantic in 1964 was the sole three-huller in the second OSTAR: *Folatre*, sailed by Derek Kelsall, who later became famous when he won the 1966 Round

Britain Race in the 42 ft trimaran *Toria* of his own design. My trimaran builders in Great Yarmouth built the three hulls, which were from another Piver design (the 35′ × 20′ × 2′6″ Lodestar class, identical to *Ultima Ratio*), but Kelsall completed *Folatre*'s construction in Kent by joining the hulls and flush-decking them over without fitting the usual coachroofs. The result, I am told, could have made a perfect helicopter landing platform. (Donald Crowhurst incorporated this idea in his Piver-designed AA. 41 class ketch *Teignmouth Electron.*)

In the same race were David Lewis' 40 ft catamaran *Rehu Moana*, and Michael Butterfield's deep-keeled cat *Misty Miller*. These, too, may have been the first cats to cross the Atlantic singlehanded, but I will be perfectly frank and admit that I am not yet sure of my facts. In the event, the race started on May 23, 1964 and *Rehu Moana* finished first of the multihulls in thirty-eight and a half days. Kelsall had the misfortune to strike a piece of driftwood, or a whale, when he was five days out, and had to return to Plymouth for repairs to his rudder and daggerboard, both of which had been broken by the impact; he left again on June 19, and crossed the finishing line on July 24: a thirty-five day crossing. *Misty Miller* took fifty-three days. After this success Lewis took *Rehu Moana* around the world, westabout via the Magellan Straits, with his wife, children and a friend, Priscilla Cairns, as crew. This was the first crewed catamaran circumnavigation (1964–7).

During Lewis' voyage, an Austrian who had emigrated to Australia, Wolf Hausner, was building a 32 ft catamaran which he named *Taboo*, and in which he later completed the first cat singlehanded circumnavigation, sailing westabout via the Cape of Good Hope, England and Panama, over a period of seven years. While this voyage was progessing (as mentioned already) Nigel Tetley circumnavigated in his 40 ft trimaran *Victress*, and so became the first-ever multihull singlehander to go round—once again the coincidence of 'firsts' all being snatched up at about the same time, yet stemming from different parts of the world!

I do not know who sailed the first singlehanded trimaran or catamaran all the way across the Pacific, and so I would welcome claims; neither do I know the first solo cat across the Indian Ocean. The first solo tri, however, belonged to Tom Corkhill, an Australian, who from January 1966 to the tail end of 1967 cruised from Manly, Queensland to Durban, South Africa via the Torres Strait, Darwin, Kupang, Singapore and Mauritius—the latter passage taking sixty-two days, which included twenty-five of total calm. The Clipper class sloop *Clipper I* (25′ × 17′ × 1′4″), designed by an Australian, Hedley Nicol, sailed 11,000 miles; she was, incidentally, also the lightest displacement singlehanded yacht to cross the Indian Ocean.

As I showed with the first half-dozen solo circumnavigators, this business of 'firsts' can be extended *ad nauseum*, for virtually any voyage across an ocean can claim a record of one sort or another. As more and more people enter the singlehanded arena, so will the claims involve much greater definition. When Hugh Vihlen, an American, crossed the Atlantic from Casablanca to Miami in 1968, taking eighty-four days, in his absurdly small 5 ft 11½ in overall sloop *April Fool*, he openly admitted that he had done so to create an all-time record. He failed on his first attempt, but succeeded with his second. Presumably, if somebody manages to cross in a 5 ft 11 in overall 'yot', Vihlen will be forgotten because his record will have been automatically eliminated by half an inch.

In my opinion this type of record breaking is even more dangerous than sponsored voyages—and therefore it is another unhappy intrusion which could in due course arouse the do-gooding instincts of those people who are constantly on the lookout for anybody who is attempting the equivalent of a juvenile playing with matches. It is no concern of mine if someone chooses to commit suicide, but I'm afraid that for every person as callous as they may regard me, there are a thousand who will happily support any campaign which proclaims its interest as 'preventing unnecessary risks which may end in possible loss of life'—or ideals to that effect. Ban one loner, and it will not be long before *all* singlehanded voyages are stopped; after all, it is common knowledge that these days, with merchant ships crowding, jostling and sinking each other all over the world, the greatest risk to the solo sailor is that he may be run down while he is asleep and nobody will ever know about it. The argument goes that if radar-equipped ships can ram and sink each other, or pile themselves up on rocky shores or sandbanks in spite of all their superior equipment, a small boat on a vast ocean, though not an easy target, is an inevitable one. Watchkeeping on large ships is sometimes even more lax than that of a single-hander; *ergo* the small boat must always lose, so ban small boats as unnecessary risk-taking! Several governments have attempted to prevent yachtsmen from sailing deep-water, including New

Zealand as long ago as 1959, and Australia after some loss of life
in multihulls in the mid-sixties, but as far as I know none has yet
managed to introduce sufficient legislation to bar for all time
those who wish to sail across oceans—whether alone or in
company; whether well-prepared or suicidal.

How would present day do-gooders have regarded the German,
Franz Romer, who in 1928 completed a canoe voyage which the
Finn-men had proved possible 250 years or so before? Romer
paddled and sailed from Lisbon via Cape St Vincent to the
Canaries in seventeen days in his ketch rigged Klepper-craft
Deutcheir Sport (21'6" × 3'). Suicidal? Not really. By judicious
use of the 50 sq ft of canvas in the tiny sails, and much hard
paddling, Romer crossed the Atlantic to St Thomas in the Virgin
Islands in fifty-eight days. He made it—this suicidal voyage—
although he had to be carried ashore after arriving because two
months of sitting in one position had atrophied his legs; he
recovered after a few weeks in hospital. Then, unfortunately, he
set out for Santo Domingo and was overtaken by a hurricane.
This time he did not make it. This time his voyage *was* suicidal.

For those who believe that legislation is the only possible
method of preventing fools from drowning themselves in small
boats, I must mention Leo Ledoux, an American ice-cream
salesman, who set off on a voyage *without any boat at all*.
Launching himself from Miami Beach one moonlit night in
August 1964, he set course for the Bahamas, floating restfully on
his back and navigating by the stars. He was sighted the next
morning by a yacht, but declined offers of help as 'it wasn't going
my way.' The yacht, *Seabird*, radioed the Coast Guard, who sent
a helicopter. But although the pilot located the human raft, a
Coast Guard cutter which went out later failed to do so. Navigational problems included the opposing Gulf Stream which, though
warm, was driving Ledoux away from his target landfall. His
second night at sea, plus accurate star-sights, proved that he was
off course, so the next morning he allowed the cabin cruiser
Stardust to rescue him. After a voyage of an estimated eighty
miles, he was now only three and a half miles from the mainland,
having been afloat for exactly thirty-two hours and thirty-eight
minutes. Swimmers have been in the water for longer than this,
and probably have covered greater distances, but none of them (I
hope) ever launched themselves in lieu of a boat. That Ledoux
had twice been in a mental institution should prove to do-gooders
that no amount of honest-to-goodness legislation will ever en-

tirely prevent suicidal voyages in yachts—or whatever!

Hannes Lindemann, another German, was seemingly as suicide-bent as his compatriot Romer, when he sailed and paddled the $23'6'' \times 2'6''$ mahogany dugout canoe *Liberia II* across the Atlantic from Las Palmas to Christiansted, St Croix between October 26 and December 28, 1955, and thence on to Haiti, from where he presented this second transatlantic dugout vessel (after Voss' *Tilikum*) to President Tubman of Liberia, presumably with thanks to the Kru tribesmen who had built it.

Undeterred by hardship (masochists abound in the small boat world), Lindemann then purchased *Liberia III*, a 17 ft 1 in Klepper, and he sailed and paddled this smallest ever canoe over much the same route, departing from Las Palmas on October 20 and arriving at St Martin on December 30, 1956. This time he took seventy-one days, against sixty-three by dugout the year before.*

It is easy to sneer at such voyages, but I suspect that Lindemann had as much purpose behind his efforts as Alain Bombard had had in 1952. Bombard, a French doctor, had departed from Casablanca on August 24, taking ten days to reach Las Palmas; he left there on October 19 and arrived at Barbados on December 23—and this time the journey was made in *L'Hérétique*, a $15' \times 6'$ rubber dinghy. His object had been to prove that shipwrecked mariners could live for months on plankton and fish. 'For forty-three days I drank only fish juice, and for the sixty-five days which the voyage lasted I lived exclusively on what I could catch from the sea. I lost fifty-five pounds in weight.'

Lindemann admitted 'I lost forty-four pounds . . .' and, like Bombard, 'I carried no fresh water; what fish I speared I ate raw' (but he had 80 kilos of concentrated food and liquid on board, the latter mostly evaporated milk and canned beer, whereas Alain Bombard had carried only sealed emergency rations). However, in all fairness I believe that Lindemann was studying more accurately than Bombard the mental processes involved in successful survival. He wrote: 'It was not until I learned something of voodoo in Haiti that I began to give really serious consideration to my new plan. Through voodoo I learned that one can, by

---

*After *Liberia III*, Lindemann had *Liberia IV* built in Hamburg in 1958. She is a conventional yacht, and no doubt Lindemann was grateful for the additional comfort when he crossed the Atlantic in her to Miami. There he sold her to Frank Casper, who renamed her *Elsie* and who went on to sail her, mostly singlehanded, around the world.

deep concentration inducing a kind of self-hypnosis, change one's fundamental attitude towards a problem...whereby one concentrates to such a point of relaxation that the environment is forgotten and the self is found.'

Although a great many books have been published in recent years about magic, mysticism, parapsychology, ESP and allied disciplines, the gap which exists between these esoteric theories and the granite facts of survival in action has never properly been bridged. Wizards, witches, shamans, Zen Buddhists and other explorers generally lack the ability to test their beliefs by life-or-death experiment, or probably more accurately, nearly all of them lack both ability and belief through inexperience of action. That Lindemann survived two Atlantic crossings against almost impossible odds must mean something, and I suspect that one day it will. The American occultist William Seabrook, who certainly participated in many dangerous adventures during his lifetime, has some interesting things to say on the subject of introversion in connection with yacht voyaging in his book *Witchcraft* (1942): Part 3, Section 2, 'Astral body on a boat'.

I have for many years used such methods while enduring long and difficult watches ashore, in the air or at the helm, and my book *East Coast Passage* describes a non-stop, fifty-nine hour stint at the wheel of my barge. This particular form of survival I have called 'helmsman's trance', which may sound to some a little more realistic than 'astral body'. Call it by any name you like, I can produce adequate evidence that I have survived so many close-to-death incidents that luck or coincidence can be disregarded as explanations. I am perfectly prepared to believe that a great deal of information could be obtained from the experiences of *every* singlehander who undoubtedly risks his or her life whenever a voyage is attempted. In due course perhaps the scientists will get around to studying this subject. In the meantime, a reading of Colin Wilson's *The Occult* (Hodder & Stoughton, 1971), and an understanding of 'Faculty X', may be helpful to potential lone sailors.

Romer's was the first canoe, and Lindemann's the smallest canoe across the Atlantic since the Finn-men; Bombard's was the first inflatable dinghy (and certainly not the last). So whose was the first raft?

This record goes to another Frenchman, René Lescombe, who was certainly an adventurer of the old school, having hunted tigers and elephants in India, parachuted into Indo-China and

138

otherwise demonstrated that he was a man of action. As is very often the case with loners, he had had wife trouble, so in 1957 he decided to cross the Atlantic on a raft. I don't think he realized that if he succeeded he would be a 'first', since he knew absolutely nothing about boats.

He wrecked his first raft after a twelve day passage. The second, *Pot-au-noir*, lasted for nine days before it broke up in a storm, and he spent another five days on the disintegrating wreckage until he was rescued. His third raft *Pot-au-noir II*, took all his money, but in the spring of 1959, short of supplies and with almost no navigational equipment, he departed from the Canary Islands for the West Indies.

This voyage of survival is even more remarkable than the canoes and inflatable dinghy achievements. Virtually foodless, Lescombe drifted into the weed-strewn clutches of the Sagasso Sea where his raft was totally becalmed for two weeks. He realized then that in spite of all his desperate efforts to feed himself from the sea, he was starving to death. Eventually he arrived at Barbados: a black bearded, sunken eyed, skin blackened sleleton of a man, barely able to stumble ashore as his raft was shattered to tiny fragments on the coral rocks off Fall In Cove on the east side of the island. But he was the first across on a raft—in fifty days! (He was last seen on his raft *1000-Bournes*, on May 26, 1963 when he spoke a Greek cargo ship; on June 8 a Portuguese fishing boat out of the Azores spotted the thing breaking up in a bad gale and tried to reach it, but the heavy seas made the task impossible. René Lescombe had made his last passage.)

Raft voyages were commonplace after *Kon-Tiki* chalked up her world famous 'first' in the South Seas. By the time Lescombe had beaten the Atlantic, no fewer than five rafts had crossed the Pacific: *Seven Little Sisters, Cantuta I, Tahiti Nui I, Tahiti Nui II, Cantuta II*. The first of these was also the first-ever singlehanded raft voyage: William Willis, raft drifter extraordinary who, aged sixty, worked his vessel 6700 miles from Callao, Peru to Samoa in 122 days (June 22 to October 12, 1954), beating the *Kon-Tiki* expedition in both distance and time. The story, *The Epic Voyage of the 'Seven Little Sisters'*, or *The Gods were Kind* (in America), is too well known for me to elaborate. His second singlehanded transpacific raft crossing was during 1963, when he again drifted from Callao to Samoa, and continued on the next year to Australia.

Willis was another mind-over-matter believer, and there is no doubt that he must have had incredible stamina to survive his various voyages. In 1966 he attempted to cross the Atlantic in his 11 ft 6 in dinghy *The Little One*; he was rescued by the US Coast Guard after sixty days, suffering from acute hernia. Again in 1967 he was rescued by a Polish trawler after three months at sea in *The Little One*—but still 1500 miles from his destination. On September 20, 1968 his dismasted boat was found by a Russian trawler 330 miles west of Ireland. The last entry in Willis' log was dated July 18, and the last day crossed off his calendar was July 20. He had set out from Montauk Point, Long Island, New York on May 1. He was seventy-four.

This two-month, uncontrolled drift by *The Little One* is by no means a record for a deserted yacht. We have seen at the beginning of this book how two Tahitians drifted in a small dinghy for 155 days, and how Poon Lim survived 133 days on a Carley Float. These times are as nothing to the extraordinary crewless voyage of the 30 ft Nimble class trimaran *Washkish*, which wandered around the Pacific in 1966–7. The description is from my book *Trimaran Development* (1972).

> She was discovered on a reef in the Lau Group of islands, Fiji, with sails part set and everything on board in good order—apart from having no crew. She had a Californian registration, and a check produced the astonishing news that the owner, Jim McCutcheon, was safe and well in America. His story was almost unbelievable.
>
> He had bought *Washkish* in San Francisco, from where he had sailed to the Marquesas. Here, he had left his crew on an island for a spell ashore. He was sailing alone at night, half asleep, when he found himself suddenly dumped into the water by a wave which seemingly had broken across the decks. Luckily his dinghy was washed off with him, and he managed to paddle ashore in this. Several weeks later, having given up all hope of seeing his tri again, he obtained a passage home.
>
> Seven months later, and 2300 miles away as the crow flies, *Washkish* made her landfall—and managed even to do that without suffering excessive damage, which is more than some tri skippers can claim. Nobody will even know how many storms she fought in those seven months.

To the best of my knowledge this is the longest shore-to-shore drift, in both time and distance, by a crewless yacht; surviving the multitudinous possibilities of disaster with very little damage must also constitute a record.

I cannot confirm the next report of the longest ever drift in a perfectly *navigable* yacht, but I suppose it is possible; single-handers are liable to do some rather weird things once they find themselves alone at sea.

On August 16, 1959 a forty-three year old New Zealander, Patrick Moore, departed from Rarotonga in the Cook Islands towards Wellington, New Zealand in his 30 ft cutter *Drifter*. On March 6, 1960 he sailed into Auckland, claiming that he had been lost for all those seven months—the last two of which he had spent in Cook Strait trying to find his position so that he could get into Wellington (which is on the north shore of Cook Strait at its narrowest part—some fifteen miles or more from South Island, depending on direction). I quote this 'record'—but refrain from further comment.

Compare such frivolity with the dedicated earnestness of Fred Rebell, the first singlehander to cross the Pacific from Australia to America (but bear in mind that it had been done fifty-one years before in the other direction by Bernard Gilboy in an 18 ft open boat).

The name Fred Rebell was invented by this Latvian (whose real name was Paul Sproge) in order to obtain a seaman's book and a passport out of the Russian militaristic and bureaucratic hell which ruled his country in pre-World War I days. A pacifist, with a longing for freedom from oppression, in 1907 Rebell stowed away on a ship going to Australia. As a settler in this new country he was given a plot of bare scrubland in the Western Territory to turn into a farm, and in due course succeeded in this task. Then he wanted to acquire a wife, so he advertised in Latvia; eventually he married Lonie, whom he had selected from thirty applicants. They had one boy, Paulie, but the marriage was not a success and they parted after twelve years. Rebell then fell for Elaine, a nineteen year old Australian, but although he loved her dearly his courtship was not very successful. She spurned him. Then the great depression of the thirties hit Sydney, where Rebell had been working as a carpenter, and he found himself out of work in company with thousands of others. While the majority clamoured for the government to do something to help their plight, Rebell decided to emigrate to the USA. The American Consul gave him little encouragement: waiting lists ... visas ... immigration laws ... But Rebell had overcome such difficulties when he had left his homeland, and he was not deterred.

He bought a clinker-built, three-quarter decked, 18 ft centreboard sloop for £20, which was all the savings he had left. Finding a job building seaside cottages at the grossly underpaid rate of £1·50 per week, he managed to save some money—enough to buy provisions for the projected voyage. He strengthened his boat by doubling the ribs and fixing an outside keel; he made a folding canvas hood to be fitted amidships for shelter; he packed dried food into old paraffin cans fitted with screw caps, and took on board 30 gallons of water. He taught himself to navigate by studying in the Sydney Public Library, and then, because navigation instruments were too expensive, he actually *made* a sextant and a distance-run log, and purchased two cheap watches which he carefully rated. His charts were all traced from an elderly atlas in the library, so ancient that later he 'discovered' islands which had been unknown when the atlas was printed. He named his yacht *Elaine*.

He left Sydney on December 31, 1931 and after a great many desperate adventures, including riding out a hurricane, he arrived at Los Angeles on January 7, 1933. The voyage of nearly 9000 miles in an open boat had taken exactly one year and one week. The total cost, including boat, food and *everything*, came to £45. He did not even have to pay for a passport, since he issued his own: 'The bearer of this passport, Fred Rebell, of no allegiance, is travelling from Sydney, Australia via Pacific Ocean, United States of America and Atlantic Ocean to his native town, Windau, in the country of Latvia. Description of bearer: Sex, male. Age: 46 years. Height 5 ft 8 in. Eyes: blue. Complexion: fair. Dated this 3 March, 1932.'

This is the kind of dedication which will not admit to the impossibility of anything. *This* is the stuff singlehanders are made of. Not like all those who rattle at the bars of security and declare that they too could achieve such results 'if only ...'.

I doubt if Rebell thought very much about the possibility of his being the first singlehanded voyager eastwards across the Pacific—any more than Ed Miles, who was at the same time crossing in *Sturdy II* from Yokohama to San Francisco (again as remarkable a coincidence as Rebell and Gilboy making their voyages in small boats of a similar size).

Those who are determined to break speed records seem to come into a different classification altogether. Most of them, it seems, need an additional challenge to the mere crossing of an ocean.

The fastest singlehanded passage eastwards across the Atlantic, from Bedford Basin, Halifax, Nova Scotia to Ireland, and later on to Scotland, is still held to this day by J V T McDonald, a Scottish master boatbuilder employed on constructing the large sailing schooners which during World War I brought food, fuel and other supplies across the Atlantic for Britain and Europe. (In World War II steam and diesel vessels of 9500–10,500 tons, known as Liberty Ships, performed the same task.) In 1922, sailing alone in his 38 ft ketch *Inverarity*, McDonald set up the all-time record of only sixteen days for the passage, as the clipper *Emerald* had done in the opposite direction nearly a century before over a longer distance.

Although the fastest time is more likely in an eastward direction, thanks to help from the Gulf Stream, most challengers seem to have preferred the warmer, westward Trade Wind crossing from the Canaries or the Cape Verde Islands towards the West Indies. In 1955 the 26 ft home-built sloop *Marta*, crewed by two Italians, Frank Rocchi and Vincent Iacopucci, crossed from the Cape Verde Islands to Brazil in seventeen days. They had departed from Viareggio, near Florence, in June 1954, and finally arrived at Baltimore, Maryland on April 5, 1957. In 1956 John Goodwin (British) in a 25 ft 3 in Vertue class sloop *Speedwell of Hong Kong* crossed in twenty-five days, and in 1962 Bill Howell (Australian) took a day less for the same passage from Las Palmas to Barbados in his 30 ft 7 in Bermudan cutter *Stardrift* (which was afterwards sailed around the world by Nicholas Clifton). In 1967 Bernard Rhodes (British) sailed the same route in a trimaran of his own design, which he had built the previous year—the 22 ft sloop *Kris*; he reduced the singlehanded time to twenty days. In 1970 Sir Francis Chichester attempted a 4000 mile run from Portuguese Guinea to Nicaragua in twenty days (i.e. averaging 200 m.p.d.) in his new, 57 ft *Gipsy Moth V*, but failed by two and one-third days, having achieved a remarkable average for a monohull of 171·9 m.p.d. over $22\frac{1}{3}$ days. In the 1972 OSTAR Alain Colas crossed from Plymouth to Newport in his 70 ft trimaran ketch *Pen Duick IV* by the more difficult direct route in twenty days, thirteen hours and fifteen minutes.

The current, fastest ever times for crewed yachts crossing the Atlantic are as follows.

In 1905 the schooner *Atlantic* sailed from Sandy Hook to the Lizard in twelve days, four hours. The nearest modern equivalent was claimed by a Dutch entrant in the 1972 OSTAR,* Gerard Dijkstra, whose Ocean 71 Bermudan ketch *Second Life* (71' × 17' × 8') unfortunately was dismasted during the westward crossing. On the return passage after the race in 1973, with an adequate crew, she sailed from Nantucket Light to Bishop Rock in the Scillies in fourteen days, thirteen hours—rather more than two days eight hours slower than the crewed three-master, which still retains the yacht transatlantic speed record for the west-to-east crossing. In the opposite direction, in 1968 the 70 ft trimaran *Pen Duick IV*, then owned and skippered by Frenchman Eric Tabarly with a crew of two, sailed from Tenerife in the Canary Islands to Martinique in the very fast time of ten days, twelve hours, averaging 253·8 m.p.d. This is the fastest ever average for any yacht in either direction, and it was during this passage that *Pen Duick IV* covered 930 nautical miles in seventy-two hours, averaging 310 m.p.d.

Although all the figures quoted in the last paragraph were for crewed yachts, I hope I have demonstrated the many difficulties involved when deciding who was 'fastest' over any particular stretch of ocean. Equally, I trust I have indicated the near impossibility of ever being sure who did what before whom. Even the blurb on the jacket of the book about Fred Rebell's voyage, *Escape to Sea* (1939), managed to get things just as wrong then as they are so often mistakenly quoted now: 'No other comparable singlehanded voyage in a small open boat' the blurb writer announced triumphantly, 'is known in history.'

You, I hope, have learned a little more about small boat history than *he* had.

I will finish this chapter with an up-to-date report of a remarkable recent survival episode by a trimaran which, although not claimed as a record, could easily have been considered as such.

On October 29, 1973 a 30 ft trimaran, *Clansman*, was towed into Whangarei Basin, North Island, New Zealand. She was badly

---

*The ridiculousness of racing across the Atlantic can be summed up adequately from the monohull handicap system which declared the 26' × 7'7" × 3'4" twin-keel Kingfisher Bermudan sloop *Blue Smoke* (Guy Hornett), the winner on handicap in the impossible time of seven days, seven hours, six minutes. She actually finished twenty-second in an elapsed time of thirty-six days, twenty-one hours, twenty-six minutes, but she had been rated a slow boat on the basis of her twin-keel configuration.

holed in the main hull and the starboard float, and her decks were awash—but she did not sink. Some thirty-six hours before, her owner Gerald Hunter (aged sixty-eight) and six friends, who were on a weekend fishing trip, had allowed *Clansman* to drift too close to the rocks off the Hen and Chickens Islands—and this was how the trimaran was damaged. Although they were some fifteen miles from the mainland, all six passengers decided to abandon ship: three men rowed back towards the shore in an aluminium dinghy, and two girls (aged nineteen and thirty) and one man (aged fifty-one) drifted about for twenty-three hours in a 6 ft inflatable dinghy until they were finally spotted by a pilot from the local flying club, who directed a launch to pick them up. Hunter very wisely stayed with his yacht. 'The skipper had more faith in the tri than we had,' one of the survivors said afterwards. 'He was quite sure it wouldn't sink, but we thought it was safer to make for the shore.'

Hunter, alone in his waterlogged tri, took the only possible chance to get her back to her home port: he hoisted sail and headed her towards the distant mainland. In due course, after being becalmed all night, he was spotted by a fisherman out of Taurikura who towed him back to Whangarei.

Not a particularly exciting adventure after all the merry mayhem we have examined, but a very rare recorded example of a completely waterlogged boat being *sailed* in order to save the life of the crew. Rare—although Captain Hosmer of the *Janet* did exactly the same thing in 1849 when his whaleboat capsized while towing a catch towards the mother ship (Chapter 3).

I don't know nearly as much about this subject as I would like, but we can be quite certain of one rule when sorting out small boat records: there is nothing new under the sun.

10
The Last Freedom

In the years following Chichester's circumnavigation, I tried very hard to penetrate the hard shells of determined ad-men who were concerned only with the voyages which they were supporting, and cared little about whatever genuine facts I was able to quote. It seemed to me that they were all going slightly crazy with their publicity—and their claims. For example, the souvenir brochures of both Chichester's and Blyth's 'historic' and 'unique' voyages (for which epistles neither man was responsible) contained route maps which indicated that the tracks went south of four Capes and five Capes respectively. In fact, as I have shown, they really went south of only three Capes and four Capes respectively. It was during this period that I received some rather rude letters which claimed that I was quibbling.

By this time the matter of records was beginning to get out of hand, mainly because nobody had ever bothered to establish the real facts—in Britain, America, or, as far as I know, anywhere. Even the Slocum Society, which had been formed for this very purpose, were unable to supply an accurate list of every known singlehanded circumnavigation. In the circumstances, I suppose my lone voice could only be accepted as a quibble—and I must admit that at the time even I did not realize that at least *twenty* singlehanded circumnavigators had set out before Chichester; I am quite sure that he did not realize this either.

I have tried to show that the evolution of singlehanded voyaging almost certainly began as accidental self-survival; that it was developed on the eastern side of the Atlantic mostly by

yachtsmen, and on the western side by publicity-seeking adventurers; and how it gradually expanded to the warm inducement
written by Joshua Slocum, with later encouragements from
others. For a time, amateur adventurers enjoyed exploring this
lonely world which they had discovered, and the 1920s and 30s
were undoubtedly their happiest years. Then came World War II,
and the dream very nearly died. It was resurrected into instant
possibilities by Thor Heyerdahl and his crew on the balsa raft
Kon-Tiki, so that many people who had never heard of old Josh
Slocum began to dream about building a raft or something and
drifting away from it all . . . The fifties was a good decade for
dreamers.

The 1960 OSTAR heralded the encroachment of professional
sponsorship into what had been almost entirely a happy amateur
sport. As publicity increased, so were the public swayed into
discussing the pros and cons of whether men should risk their
lives sailing small boats across oceans. The 1968 OSTAR, and the
air searches for such newsworthy entrants as Joan de Kat, and
Edith Baumann and her pet dog (who had to be rescued when her
40 foot trimaran *Koala* began to break up), began the inevitable
inrush of do-gooding by indefatigable savers of other people's
lives and/or souls. Now *everybody* knew about small boat adventuring; now *everybody* wanted to get into the act in one way or
another; now *everybody* was ready to express an opinion.

When Drake completed his circumnavigation Queen Elizabeth
I knighted him, after a struggle with her conscience. When
Schouten rounded Cape Horn, the Dutch East India Company
condemned him until he managed to prove that he had not been
guilty of any wrongdoing. Pirates and privateers were sponsored
by lords and ladies and various other gentry, which gave an
infamous trade a spurious legality. After Baré was 'exposed' she
became the heroine of the French public; in the same manner, the
female pirates Read and Bonny have been romanticized far
beyond the sordid facts which were revealed at their trial. Oh,
how the general public have so often proved their gullibility by
accepting, without question, propaganda and very nearly anything else they are are told 'officially'. And now they are presented, at least for a time, with sponsored 'yacht' voyages, and all
that this implies.

'And what,' you may well ask, 'is so very terrible about
promoting such events?'

The answer lies in the degree of do-gooding which sponsorship invokes. In the past nobody paid much attention to the thousands of small boat escapers, and certainly the public were never over bothered whenever somebody was posted missing, or a wrecked yacht was discovered. Besides, in the years up until the 1960s very few of the singlehanders were interested actually in breaking records: most were on the high seas for various personal reasons quite unconnected with record breaking, although if they *did* happen to achieve a 'first' or a 'fastest' during the process it was invariably accepted as a small gift from the gods, which might in due course produce a little extra cash to tide one over the next bad period.

As I have pointed out earlier, sponsored voyages imply maximum possible effort by those involved. The promoters, by the very nature of sponsorship, must extract maximum publicity before, during and (if successful) after the voyage. So a larger percentage of public interest is automatically involved, whereas few people know about an unsponsored sailor until *after* a voyage, and not necessarily then. This means that if the sponsored skipper gets into difficulties, the media is on to it like a shot—with all the pros and cons being discussed by 'experts', do-gooders and the propagandized public. Result: invariably more rules and regs to harrass the individual who is quietly going about his own business, in his own time, risking only his own life and trying very hard to interfere as little as possible with anybody. So why *should* sponsors be allowed to help ruin this last escape to freedom?

Perhaps I plead too much for a lost cause, for it is not only sponsors who have brought about this disintegration of freedom for individual sea adventure.

Pollution of the oceans of the world by developed and developing countries is too well known. Sailors have always risked death at sea, but generally only because of the simple forces of nature. Now they face additional and unrecognizable perils—such as fish and water poisoned by mankind, and the very atmosphere—those wonderful, cool Trade Winds, or the frightening, screaming gales in the far south—which carry the terrible possibility of a lingering death from radiation or the other spores of hell which are released by the continuing mad desire of scientists to experiment, or by uncontrolled industry.

So I doubt if it is a coincidence that such circumnavigators as Walter König, a German, developed leukemia, and Leonid Teliga, a Pole, suffered agonies from cancer of the stomach, both of which progressively grew worse, so that König died two months after his arrival home and Teliga about a year after completing his circumnavigation. These are but two examples; I suspect there have been, and will be, more.

The French selected Mururoa for testing their nuclear bombs. Fletcher Christian's utopia, Pitcairn Island (which became a worse hell on earth than all his experiences under Captain Bligh, and in the Royal Navy), lies 530 miles to the southeast of Mururoa, on the fringe of the danger zone. Other islands, too, are in the same terrible position, but all the world knows about Bligh and Christian—and Pitcairn.

Chauvinist de Gaulle approved the test area, and was happy enough when the first thermonuclear device was exploded there in 1966. This was the *force de frappe* he had promised the French people. Nobody took much notice of the Pitcairners, who since that day have been subjected to this unholy terror for four months in each year, and to its long-term effects continuously. They have no alternative, for how can a total population of eighty-five defend its rights against the French government? So radioactive rain now falls from time to time on Pitcairn and surrounding waters, and the British and Americans have instruments there which tell them that the Pitcairners should leave their paradise-on-earth: but they don't want to go—and why should they?

Of course the British and the Americans have been as guilty in the past as the French are now. Another Schouten-versus-mighty combine type of battle was fought in those earlier days by the American yachtsman Dr Earle Reynolds, backed by his wife Barbara, his two children Jessica and Ted, and his crew Nick Mikami (who, incidentally, became the first Japanese to circumnavigate in a yacht when this 54,000 mile voyage in Reynold's 50 ft ketch *Phoenix* was finally completed). In brief, the US Atomic Energy Commission had declared some 390,000 square miles of the Pacific prohibited to shipping of all nations while tests were in progress. Reynolds sailed into this area and was promptly arrested. Tried in Honolulu, he was found guilty, but a subsequent appeal to a higher court was successful—after a considerable and unnecessary expenditure of personal money and time. The US Court of Appeals at San Francisco ruled that their Atomic Energy Commission did *not* have the right to commandeer vast areas of the high seas for their experiments, and reversed the Honolulu conviction. Unfortunately the French seem not imbued with similar objectivity, and so every sailor now has to consider this additional, invisible peril of the sea when crossing the Pacific.

Other diseases and injuries are more natural risks, which solo and short-handed sailors accept. Most yachtsmen generally take a good medicine chest and instructions and hope for the best. But what of total incapacitation when a man is alone on his boat? There have been some grisly stories told on this subject.

Vito Dumas, shortly after setting out on his circumnavigation, discovered that *Lehg II* was leaking. During the long and difficult process of shifting his stores about the yacht to discover the source, he bruised and cut both his hands. Five days after leaving Montevideo his right arm became infected, and with bandages on both hands he was unable to do very much to help himself or his yacht. His temperature rose as his right arm and hand swelled; later he became feverish. The pain gradually worsened until it was unbearable. He gave himself an injection: he was now shivering with fever and sick with apprehension. He no longer cared if *Lehg II* survived the gales which had been battering at her for the three, four, five days—he was not sure—that the ghastly pain had tormented him. He had to decide that on the very next day he would amputate his obscene arm, already smelling of decay and dragging him to death with it. Worn out by the ceaseless violent tossing of his boat, lack of sleep, overwhelming worry about his arm, intense pain, what would happen to him after he had performed an amputation, his lack of medical knowledge, the high fever, the leak which he had stemmed temporarily, bad weather . . . he lost consciousness. He awoke many hours later to find that it was past midnight of the seventh day of his suffering—and that he was lying in a stinking morass of his own pus. There was a three inch gaping hole in his arm. Somehow he had burst the wound as he writhed in unconscious pain. Slowly, as the days passed, he recovered from this appalling experience, and continued his struggle to complete this first voyage in the Roaring Forties.

The risks which singlehanders take whenever they put to sea must be far beyond the understanding of any landlubber, who probably thinks that gales—or at worse, hurricanes—are the ultimate evil.

Jean Gau, after visiting his birthplace at Valras Plage, France towards the end of his first circumnavigation, left there on May 26, 1957 for Gibraltar and Funchal on Maderia, departing on July

17 for New York. On September 21 Hurricane Carrie enwrapped Gau's 30 ft Tahiti ketch *Atom* and the 3103 ton, four-masted barque *Pamir* in all the fury of her whirling 120 m.p.h. wind. *Pamir* lost the fight almost at the start: sails, yards, sheets and braces thrummed and became as rigid as steel; blocks jammed; canvas burst; rigging parted; t'gallant and topmasts crashed to the deck. *Pamir* broached, listed to 45°: then her cargo shifted. In thirty seconds, according to a survivor, she rolled right over and went down like a submarine. Of the crew of thirty-five professional seamen and fifty-one young German cadets, only six persons were saved!

Gau arrived at Sheepshead Bay, Brooklyn on October 3. Asked how he had survived a storm which had brought almost instant death to a mighty square-rigger, he was reported as saying: 'Before it struck I just furled all sails, lashed the helm down, rigged a can so it dripped oil overside to keep the seas from breaking. Then I closed myself in the cabin and slept, ate, read and drew pictures.' It is not always as easy as that, but Gau's studied nonchalance gives some indication that storms are not necessarily the worst hazard which the loner must face at sea.

I have not met Jean Gau, but I have read descriptions of him, and from meeting other singlehanders it seems that although the breed can be broadly divided into 'voyagers' and 'record breakers', they are surprisingly similar in their dedication.

We have seen how Brendan pursued his voyages until he was satisfied that he had accomplished whatever task he had mentally set himself. Pirate and privateer commanders did the same; Schouten fought to prove the authenticity of the facts he had gathered; Magellan died rather than give up the chance of converting the heathen; Drake organized his Queen to get what he wanted. And in more recent times we have seen similar dedication in nearly every singlehander. These people were, and still are, very much in a class of their own, and the extraordinary thing is that this very rare trait has never been properly recognized—except by those sponsors who have exploited it over the centuries, notably during times of war.

Sharon Sites showed this determination from a slightly different aspect, in a letter to me in January 1974. 'I have tried several times to find another boat so I could cross the Atlantic, but to no avail. Now I have reached the age (and financial state) where I have to give up my adventures, and accepting challenges of that nature. I have recently started in the world of banking to face the challenge of moving up the ladder to a managerial position. I guess I must always have a challenge. I wouldn't change the last ten years for anything, but I am envious of those who have capitalized on their exploits enough so they can continue sailing.'

And there you have it: money has to come from somewhere, which these days generally involves sponsorship of one sort or another. Lack of funds is nearly always the main excuse offered by the majority; they can be heard at any boat show claiming fervently that they 'would love to have a go, if only . . .'. Those last two words are probably the most self-convincing, non-argument cliché in the English language: If only I wasn't married . . . If only I had the time . . . If only I didn't have so many responsibilities . . . If only I wasn't up to my ears in mortgage . . . If only I could build a boat like that . . .

Yet Donald Ridler built a boat 'like that' in 1969. At the time he had £250 in the bank, and an overpowering desire to cross an ocean, singlehanded, in his own craft. He obtained the plans of a 26 ft ketch designed by John T Rowland of Maine in 1946 on the lines of an American Cape Anne dory, and he solved the if-only problems as he worked with his hands and began to live. He taught himself to sail *Eric the Red* by the same relentless process.

I do not necessarily endorse this method as being the best, but if one succeeds he has certainly been thoroughly indoctrinated in the first and most important rule which anyone must clearly understand when battling against Nature: kill or be killed. To translate, and point out that by 'kill' I mean that all opposition, including Nature, must be beaten, overcome, eliminated or eradicated, rather spoils the impact; 'kill or be killed' is the rule, and however you like to temper the first part I can assure you that Nature seldom softens her response.

So Ridler built his boat with unskilled hands for £205. Food to last for six months and navigational equipment cost him a further £80. He set forth to cross the Atlantic with £20 in his pocket— plus £50 in traveller's cheques, which was his sole reserve. He planned, as so many do, on earning money at odd jobs on the way.

His double crossing of the Atlantic was entirely successful. He left Falmouth on May 10, 1970, cruising via Gibraltar and the Canaries to Barbados, where he arrived on November 18. From there, visiting many of the wonderful Windward and Leeward Islands, he went on to Bermuda, arriving on June 29, 1971 and departing six days later. Calling at the Azores on the way home, he finally arrived back in Falmouth on September 24—out of food (apart from two soup cubes), with no fuel for cooking (apart from some remnants of candle dripping), and hardly any money. But no longer was he an unhappy member of the if-only brigade. The details of how such things can be accomplished on a very short shoestring are in his book *Eric the Red* (Kimber, 1972).

Although Donald Ridler did not break any records, I have mentioned his adventure as a contra-example to the very expensive sponsored voyages which seem to have taken over the ocean cruising and ocean racing scene. Now you know that it *is* possible for you, and you, and you to go to sea in your own boat. You don't *have* to have a million-pound organization behind you to enjoy this kind of adventure, this freebooting, this last freedom which is so rapidly disappearing. You don't *have* to, but it does seem that an awful lot of people prefer it.

I have done my best to give some semblance of order to the evolution of singlehanded voyagers in small boats. On looking back over what I have written I realize that there are far too many gaps, mainly because information is either sparse, non-existent, or too expensive for me to research at present. The appendices which follow are, as far as I can discover, the first comprehensive lists ever to be published on this subject. I regret only that they are not yet comprehensive enough.

All that is left is for me to expose the one thought which every singlehander should always consider, but seldom does until it is too late. I quote from my book *The Lure of the Sea.*

> To the genuine loner, illness or accident to self is the greatest hazard, and there have been some cases of death. There are always greater risks in going it alone, rather than sharing your experiences with others, yet I feel sure that those who really want to be alone can face even old age and the final blanking off of life with equanimity. Perhaps they have found something at sea which is denied to land-bound rat-racers; perhaps they are not really lonely at all? So the final analysis of whether you are a natural singlehander is really just that one question: could you face dying alone?

> 'In the morning of June 13, 1891 Mr McMullen landed and posted a letter at Eastbourne. After this he boarded the *Perseus* again, and went on down Channel. The next heard of him was a telegram on June 16, saying he was found dead on

the evening of the 15th by some French fishermen. He was sitting in the cockpit, with his face looking towards the sky, and the vessel sailing herself along. The doctor said he had been dead twenty-four hours when his body was found, the cause of death being failure of the heart's action. He must, therefore, have died in mid-Channel on Sunday night, June 14th. The weather was fine, the breeze light, and the young moon was shimmering on the placid sea...'

Thus concluded the classic, R T McMullen's *Down Channel.*
   It is to this final conclusion that your self-analysis must aim.

Consider all such points before you finally decide to escape to sea in a small boat, and remember that there have been many unsuccessful attempts against every completed voyage. It is as well to brood about such matters in detail, introspectively and honestly, before you irrevocably commit yourself to the deep.

Adventure on, and if you suffer, swear
That the next venturer shall have less to bear;
Your way will be retrodden, make it fair.

Think, though you thunder on in might, in pride,
Others may follow fainting, without guide,
Burn out a trackway for them; blaze it wide.

And you, the gray thing dragging on the sea
Go as a man goes in Eternity
Under a crown of stars to Destiny.

from *The Ending* by John Masefield

Asterisks in the Appendices refer to the books about particular voyages; authors are listed alphabetically in the Bibliography. Other books which an author may have written are not listed, and only modern works in English editions are mentioned. This simple listing has been compiled merely for readers who wish to learn more about some of the small boat record-breakers and solo sailors.

Explanatory notes and abbreviations will be found at the end of each Appendix.

Bibliography

Adams, Sharon Sites *Interlude in Sea Sharp* (unpublished manuscript).

Allcard, Edward *Voyage Alone* (Robt Hale 1964).

Bardiaux, Marcel *Four Winds of Adventure* (de Graff; A Coles 1961).

Bernicot, Louis *The Voyage of the Anahita* (Hart-Davis 1953).

de Bisschop, Eric *Tahiti Nui* (Collins; McDowell Obolensky 1959).

Blackburn, Howard *Lone Voyager* (by Joseph E Garland) (Little, Brown; Hutchinson 1964).

Blyth, Chay *The Impossible Voyage* (Hodder & Stoughton; Putnam 1971). *Theirs is the Glory* (Hodder & Stoughton 1974).

Bombard, Alain *The Bombard Story* or *Voyage of the Hérétique* (Deutsch; Simon & Schuster 1953).

Carlin, Ben *Half-Safe* (Deutsch 1955).

Chichester, Francis *Alone Across the Atlantic* (Allen & Unwin; Doubleday 1961). *Gipsy Moth Circles the World* (Hodder & Stoughton; Coward, McCann 1967). *The Romantic Challenge* (Cassell; Coward, McCann 1971).

Davison, Ann *My Ship is So Small* (Peter Davies; Wm Sloane 1956).

Dumas, Vito *Alone Through the Roaring Forties* (de Graff; A Coles 1960).

Fairfax, John *Britannia: Rowing Alone Across the Atlantic*

(Wm Kimber; Simon & Schuster 1972). *Oars Across the Pacific* (with Sylvia Cook) (Wm Kimber; Norton 1972).

Follett, Tom *Project Cheers* (with Dick Newick and Jim Morris) (A Coles 1968).

Gerbault, Alain *Fight of the Firecrest* (Hodder & Stoughton 1926; de Graff). *In Quest of the Sun* (Hodder & Stoughton 1929; de Graff).

Gilboy, Bernard *A Voyage of Pleasure* (ed. by John Barr Tompkins) (Cornell Maritime 1956).

Graham, Robin Lee *Dove* (Harper & Row; Angus & Robertson 1972).

Guzzwell, John *Trekka Round the World* (A Coles 1963).

Hayter, Adrian *Sheila in the Wind* (Hodder & Stoughton 1959). *Business in Great Waters* (Hodder & Stoughton 1965).

Horie, Kenichi *Koduku* (Collins 1965).

King, Cdr William *Capsize* (Nautical 1969). *Adventures in Depth* (Putnam 1975).

Knox-Johnston, Robin *A World of My Own* (Cassell; Wm Morrow 1969).

Lewis, David *The Ship Would Not Travel Due West* (Hart-Davis 1963).

Le Toumelin, Jacques-Yves *Kurun Around the World* (Hart-Davis 1954).

Lindemann, Hannes *Alone at Sea* (Random House 1958).

Marin-Marie *Wind Aloft, Wind Alow* (Scribners; Peter Davies 1945).

McClean, Tom *I Had to Dare* (Jarrolds 1971).

Mermod, Michael *The Voyage of the Geneve* (John Murray 1973).

Milnes Walker, Nicolette *When I Put Out To Sea* (Collins; Stein & Day 1972).

Moitessier, Bernard *The Long Way* (A Coles; Doubleday 1974).

Peterson, Marjorie *Stornoway East and West* (Van Nostrand 1966).

Pidgeon, Harry *Around the World Singlehanded* (Appleton 1932; de Graff; Hart Davis 1960).

Rebell, Fred *Escape to the Sea* (John Murray 1939, 1951; Dodd Mead).

Ridgeway, John *A Fighting Chance* (with Chay Blyth) (Hamlyn; Lippincott 1966).

Riding, John *The Voyage of the Sea Egg*   (Pelham 1968). *Sea Egg Again*   (Pelham 1972).

Robinson, William Albert   *Deep Water and Shoal*   (Cape 1932; de Graff; Hart-Davis).

Rose, Alec *My Lively Lady* (Nautical Publishing; McKay 1968).

Slocum, Joshua *Sailing Alone Around the World*   (originally Century 1900; various publishers subsequently).

Tabarly, Eric *Lonely Victory* (Souvenir Press; Clarkson Potter 1965). *Pen Duick*   (A Coles; Norton 1971).

Tangvald, Peter *Sea Gypsy* (Dutton; Wm Kimber 1966).

Tetley, Nigel *Trimaran Solo* (Nautical 1970).

Voss, John *The Venturesome Voyages of Captain Voss* (originally Japan Herald Press, Yokohama 1913; de Graff; Hart Davis).

Williams, Geoffrey *Sir Thomas Lipton Wins* (Peter Davies; Lippincott 1969).

Willis, William *The Epic Voyage of the Seven Little Sisters* (Hutchinson 1955)   published in the USA as *The Gods were Kind*   (Dutton).

Wharram, James *People of the Sea*   (Sun & Health 1965).

The following four books give excellent general details of singlehanded ocean voyages.

Barton, Humphrey *Atlantic Adventurers*   (Van Nostrand; A Coles 1953).

Borden, Charles A *Sea Quest*   (Robt Hale 1967).

Holm, Donald *The Circumnavigators* (Prentice-Hall; Angus & Robertson 1974).

Merrien, Jean *Lonely Voyagers* (Hutchinson 1954).

Many books have been published about the four Observer Singlehanded Transatlantic Races, both personal narrative and general observation. Written just after the 1972 OSTAR, the most detailed book about all four races is:

Page, Frank *Solo to America*   (A Coles Ltd; Quadrangle/NY Times 1972).

A thorough and painstaking study of the competitors' tactics and experiences in the 1968 OSTAR, as well as an account of his own passage, is:

Pakenham, Stephen *Separate Horizons*   (Nautical 1970).

The First Circumnavigators

Ship	Flag	Captain or leader(s) of expedition
Vittoria[1]	Spain	Ferdinand Magellan (killed 1521) Juan Sebastian del Cano[1]
Golden Hind	England	Francis Drake
De Mauritius	Holland	Olivier van Noort
Eendracht	Holland	Willem Schouten (sent home from Batavia in disgrace on *Amsterdam*)
Duke and *Duchess*	Gt Britain	Woodes Rogers Stephen Courtney
Dolphin and *Tamar*	Gt Britain	John Byron
La Boudeuse *Étoile*	France	Louis Antoine de Bougainville
Union (sloop rigged)	USA	John Boit, Jr (age 19) and crew of 22 (youngest captain ever to circumnavigate)
Betsy	USA	Edmund Fanning
various (see Chap. 3)	Japan	Four seamen: Tsudayuu, Sahei, Gihei, Tajuu
Nadeshda, and *Neva*	Russia	A J Von Kruzenshtern
Mary Ann (sch.)	Sweden	Nils Werngren
Concordia	Denmark	Thomas Jepson Sodring

Sailed from	Dates	Direc-tion	Remarks
Seville	1519–22	E–W (M)	First ship to circumnavigate (18 survived to bring *Vittoria* home, from 240 in five ships that started)
Plymouth	1577–80	E–W (M)	First commander to complete voyage in own ship. First British circumnavigation.[2]
Rotterdam	1598–1601	E–W (M)	First Dutch circumnavigation
Texel	1615–17	E–W (H)	First rounding of Cape Horn
Bristol	1708–11	E–W (H)	First successful return of two-ship convoy
Deal, Kent	1764–6	E–W (M)	First voyage of scientific investigation around world
St Malo	1766–9	E–W (M)	First French circumnavigation
Newport, RI	1794–6	E–W (H)	First circumnavigation by fore-and-aft rigged vessel. First American circumnavigation
New York	1797–9	E–W (H)	First American circumnavigation by square-rigged ship
Mutsu, Japan	1793–1804	E–W (H)	First Japanese seamen to circum-navigate
Kronstadt	1803–6	E–W (H)	First Russian circumnavigation
Lulea	1839–41	E–W (H)	First Swedish circumnavigation
Copenhagen	1839–41	E–W (H)	First Danish circumnavigation

Preciosa	Norway	Carl Frederik Diriks
Hercules	Finland	Peter Gustaf Idman
Keying[3] (Chinese junk)	Gt Britain China	Charles A Kellett
Victoria	Germany	J C Godeffroy
Magenta (steam corvette)	Italy	Cdr Vittorio Arminjon

(H) via Cape Horn; (M) via Magellan Straits.

[1]The original spellings were *Victoria* and de Elcano. A carpenter, Andrews of Bristol, one of the 18 survivors, was the first Briton to sail round the world.

Drammen	1840–3	E–W (H)	First Norwegian circumnavigation
Jakobstad	1844–7	E–W (H)	First Finnish circumnavigation
Hong Kong	1846–8	E–W	Via Cape Town and New York to England. Longest junk voyage.
Hamburg	1848–9	W–E (H)	First German circumnavigation
Montevideo	1866–8	W–E (H)	First Italian circumnavigation

[2]The pirate Bartholomew Sharp was the first British captain to round Cape Horn. He sailed eastabout on a captured Spanish ship on November 15, 1681.

[3]The voyage of the *Keying* was not a circumnavigation, but is listed as it was the greatest known distance sailed by a Chinese junk. Three British officers and 12 white crew, plus a Chinese captain (compulsory under Chinese law) and 26 Chinese seamen, sailed her to New York.

Singlehanded Circumnavigations in Starting Date Order

	Name	Born/ Flag	Yacht	Length	Beam	Draft
1	Joshua Slocum*	NS/ USA	*Spray*	36' 9"	14' 2"	4' 2"
2	Harry Pidgeon*	USA	*Islander*	34'	10' 9"	5'
3	Alain Gerbault*	Fr	*Firecrest*	39'	8' 6"	7'
4	Edward Miles	USA	*Sturdy* *Sturdy II*	37' 4" .36' 9"	10' 10' 10"	4' 7" 4' 9"
5	Harry Pidgeon	USA	*Islander*	34'	10' 9"	5'
6	Louis Bernicot*	Fr	*Anahita*	41'	11' 6"	5' 7"
7	Vito Dumas*	Arg	*Lehg II*	31' 2"	10' 9"	5' 8"
8	Al Peterson*	USA	*Stornoway*	33'	11'	5' 10"
9	Marcel Bardiaux*	Fr	*Les Quatre Vents*	30' 8"	8' 10"	5' 9"
10	Adrian Hayter*	NZ/ GB	*Sheila II* *Valkyr*	32' 25'	8' 6" 7' 2"	5' 3' 9"
11	Jean Gau	Fr/ USA	*Atom*	30'	9' 10"	4' 7"

Hull	Rig	Route	Dates	Remarks
W	Gaff yawl	E–W (M)	1895–8	First solo circum-navigation (westabout)
W	Gaff yawl	E–W (P)	1921–5	First using Panama Canal during circumnavigation
W	Bm. cutter	E–W (P)	1923–9	First French solo
W	Two-masted bm. schs.	W–E (SP)	1928–32	First eastabout. First using both canals. (*Sturdy I* burnt out in Red Sea.)
W	Gaff yawl	E–W (P)	1932–7	First to circumnavigate solo twice
W	Bm. cutter	E–W (M)	1936–8	Only other solo circum'r (after Slocum) via Magellan Straits
W	Bm. ketch	W–E (H)	1942–3	First Argentinian solo. First solo eastabout round Horn.
W	Gaff cutter	E–W (PS)	1948–52	First using both canals, westabout
W	Bm. sloop	E–W (H)	1950–8	First circumnavigation after rounding Horn westabout
W	Gaff yawl Bm. sloop	W–E (S) E–W (P)	1950–6 1962–3	First New Zealand solo. Both voyages started from England to NZ.
W	Gaff ketch	E–W (P)	1953–7	

12	John Guzzwell*	GB	*Trekka*	20' 6"	6' 6"	4' 6"
13	Joseph Havkins*	Isr	*Lammerhak II*	23'	7'	4' 6"
14	Edward Allcard*	GB	*Sea Wanderer*	36'	11'	5' 4"
15	Bill Nance	Aus	*Cardinal Vertue*	25' 3"	7' 2"	4' 6"
16	Jean Gau	Fr/ USA	*Atom*	30'	9' 10"	4' 7"
17	Pierre Auboiroux	Fr	*Néo-Vent*	27'	7' 6"	4' 4"
18	Robin Lee Graham*	USA	*Dove* *Return of Dove*	24' 33'	7' 6" 9'	4' 5'
19	Rusty Webb	GB	*Flyd*	29' 3"	9' 6"	4' 9"
20	Alfred Kallies	Ger	*Pru*	25'	7' 11"	4' 1"
21	Wilfried Erdman	Ger	*Kathena*	25'	7' 7"	4' 11"
22	John Sowden	USA	*Tarmin*	24' 7"	7' 8"	4' 8"
23	Francis Chichester*	GB	*Gipsy Moth IV*	53' 1"	10' 6"	7' 9"
24	Wolf Hausner	A/ Aus	*Taboo* (cat)	32'	15'	3'
25	Leonid Teliga	Pol	*Opty*	32' 4"	9' 4"	5' 1"
26	Roger Plisson	Fr	*François Virginie*	24'	7'	4'

W	Bm. yawl	E–W (P)	1955–9	First British solo. Smallest yacht to circumnavigate.
W	Bm. yawl	E–W	1956–61	First Israeli solo. Overland Mexico and Israel.
W	Bm. ketch	E–W (H)	1957–73	Most protracted. Tied knot in Antigua.
W	Bm. sloop	W–E (H)	1962–5	First Australian solo.
W	Bm. ketch	E–W (P)	1962–8	Second to circumnavigate solo twice
W	Bm. sloop	E–W (PS)	1964–6	
G	Bm. sloops	E–W (P)	1965–70	Youngest, at $16\frac{1}{3}$–$21\frac{1}{6}$ years
W	Bm. sloop	E–W (P)	1965–8	Record: 84,000 miles in seven years sailing *Flyd*
W	Bm. sloop	E–W (P)	1965–9	
W	Bm. sloop	E–W (P)	1966–8	First German solo
W	Bm. sloop	E–W (P)	1966–70	
W	Bm. yawl	W–E (H)	1966–7	First with only one stopover
P	Bm. sloop	E–W (P)	1966–73	First solo catamaran. First Austrian solo.
W	Bm. yawl	E–W (P)	1967–9	First Polish solo
W	Bm. sloop	E–W (P)	1967–9	

27	Alec Rose*	GB	*Lively Lady*	36'	9' 3"	6' 8"
28	Robin Knox-Johnston*	GB	*Suhaili*	32' 5"	11' 1"	5' 6"
29	Bernard Moitessier*	IC/ Fr	*Joshua*	39' 6"	12'	5' 3"
30	Nigel Tetley*	SA/ GB	*Victress* (tri)	40'	22'	2' 9"
31	Tom Blackwell*	GB	*Islander*	58' 6"	12' 8"	7' 8"
32	Chay Blyth*	GB	*British Steel*	59'	12' 10"	8'
33	Bill King	Eire/ GB	*Galway Blazer II*	42'	10' 5"	6'
34	Jorgen Meyer	Ger	*Paloma*	34'	10'	4' 10"
35	Göran Cederström	Swed	*Tua Tua*	27' 4"	8' 3"	4' 5"
36	Hiroshi Aoki	Jap	*Ahodori II*	20' 9"	6' 8"	4' 3"
37	Kris Baranowski	Pol	*Polonez*	45' 3"	12' 5"	7' 3"
38	Alain Colas	Fr	*Manureva* (tri)	70'	35'	9'

W	Bm. yawl	W–E (H)	1967–8	
W	Bm. ketch	W–E (H)	1968–9	Record: longest time at sea solo, 313 days.
S	Bm. ketch	W–E (H)	1968–9	First solo non-stop circumnavigation. First steel hull.
P	Bm. ketch	W–E (H)	1968–9	First solo trimaran and multihull.
W	Bm. ketch	E–W (P)	1968–71	Largest singlehanded yacht to circumnavigate via Panama Canal
S	Bm. ketch	E–W (H)	1970–1	First non-stop westabout: 292 days. Largest monohull.
P	Junk-rigged two-masted sch.	W–E (H)	1970–3	First Irish solo (sailed under both flags). Rig also called 'Chinese lug'. (Apx. 4)
G	Bm. sloop	E–W (P)	1971–2	Record: fastest solo in low latitudes, 349 days
G	Bm. sloop	E–W (P)	1971–3	First Swedish solo
P	Bm. yawl	W–E (H)	1971–4	Record: smallest to round Horn. Second smallest to circumnavigate.
W	Bm. ketch	W–E (H)	1972–3	Record: Hobart to Cape Horn in 45 days. (Apx. 4)
A	Bm. ketch	W–E (H)	1973–4	Record: fastest solo, 167 days. Largest yacht, first aluminium hull.

39	Kenichi Horie*	Jap	*Mermaid III*	28' 10"	9' 3"	5' 5"
40	Ambrogio Fogar	It	*Suprise*	38' 8"	11' 2"	6' 2"
41	Ryusuke Ushijima	Jap	*Gingitsune*	31'	9' 10"	4' 7"

Flag/Born:	NS	Nova Scotia	*Hulls*:	W	wood
	A	Austria		G	fibreglass
	Aus	Australia		S	steel
	IC	Indo-China		P	ply or
	SA	South Africa			moulded wood
	Isr	Israel		A	aluminium

Rig:	Bm.	bermudan	*Route*:	(P)	via Panama Canal
	Sch.	schooner		(S)	via Suez Canal
				(M)	via Magellan Straits
				(H)	via Cape Horn

Late information just before going to press The following singlehanders completed circumnavigations in 1975, but complete details were not available for accurate listing.

Heinrich Julius Henze (Ger), 24'8" *Leda* (Steel). E–W via Panama, 1971–5.

Richard Konkolski (Czech), 24'4" yawl *Niké*. E–W via Panama, 1972–5.

John Struchinsky, 25'3" Vertue *Bonaventure de Lys*. E–W via Panama, 1972–5.

170

W	Bm. sloop	E–W (H)	1973–4	First Japanese solo. Fastest non-stop westabout, 275 days.
W	Bm. sloop	E–W (H)	1973–4	First Italian solo
W	Bm. ketch	W–E (H)	1973–4	

Singlehanded circumnavigators can be broadly divided into two classes: those who cruised around the world, and those who raced. By setting out this list in starting date order I believe I have been fair to both, although anomalies are inevitable.

Part Singlehanded and/or Near-Circumnavigations in Starting Date Order

Name	Born/ Flag	Yacht	Length	Beam	Draft
John Voss* various crew	Ger/ USA	Tilikum	38'	5' 6"	2'
William A Robinson* Etera	USA Tahiti	Svaap	32'	9' 6"	5' 7"
Bill Murnan	USA	Seven Seas II	30'	9' 8"	3'
J-Y le Toumelin*	Fr	Kurun	33'	11' 10"	5' 4"
Peter Tangvald*	Nor/ USA	Dorothea I	32'	9' 10"	6'
Michael Mermod*	Swiss	Genève	25' 7"	8' 6"	4' 11"
Ed Boden	USA	Kittywake	25' 3"	7' 2"	4' 6"
Frank Casper	USA	Elsie	29' 8"	11'	5' 6"
John Riding*	GB	Sjö Äg	12'	5' 3"	2' 3"
Alan Eddy	USA	Apogee	30' 6"	9' 3"	4' 4"
Walter König	Ger	Zarathustra	24' 9"	9' 2"	3' 7"
Nicholas Clifton	GB	Stardrift	30' 7"	8' 6"	5' 3"

Hull	*Rig*	*Route*	*Dates*	*Remarks*
W	Three-masted gaff sch.	E–W	1901–4	Indian dugout canoe 100 years old. Solo for 1500 miles, otherwise with one crew. No knot.
W	Bm. ketch	E–W (PS)	1928–31	First two-crew circumnavigation.
SS	Bm. ketch	E–W	1948–52	First stainless steel hull. Part-pass. No knot.
W	Gaff cutter	E–W (P)	1949–52	Part-pass.
W	Bm. cutter	E–W (PS)	1959–64	Part-pass.
W	Bm. sloop	E–W	1961–6	First Swiss attempt. No knot.
W	Bm. sloop	E–W (P)	1962–	Most protracted voyage after Allcard (personal claim).
W	Bm. cutter	E–W (P)	1963–6	Part-pass.
P	Bm. sloop	E–W (P)	1964–73	Smallest craft to attempt circum. Lost in Tasman Sea.
G	Bm. ketch	E–W (P)	1965–9	First fibreglass hull. Part-pass.
G	Bm. sloop	E–W (P)	1965–9	Part-pass. Bypassed Suez, overland to Israel.
W	Bm. cutter	E–W (P)	1966–73	Part-pass.

173

Rollo Gebhard	Ger	*Solveig III*	24' 4"	7' 10"	4' 3"
Ulf Peterson	Swed	*Suzie II*	35' 9"	9'	4' 11"
Graeme Dillon	GB	*Mayfly*	30'	10'	5'

Hulls: W wood   *Rig*: Bm. bermudan
        SS stainless steel   Sch. schooner
        P ply or moulded wood
        G fibreglass

Route: (P) via Panama Canal
        (S) via Suez Canal
        (H) via Cape Horn

W	Bm. sloop	E–W (P)	1967–70	Part-pass.
G	Bm. sloop	E–W (P)	1968–74	Part-pass.
W	Gaff cutter	E–W (P)	1971–4	Part-pass. Ex-oyster dredger, built 1902.

Remarks: *Part-pass*: one passenger or crew was carried for part of the voyage.   *No knot*: homeward course did not cross outward track.

Singlehanded Cape Horners

	Name	Born/ Flag	Yacht	Length	Beam	Draft
Two crew	George Blythe Peter Arapakis	GB Gk/ Aus	*Pandora*	36' 9"	14' 2"	4' 2"
1	Al Hansen	Nor	*Mary Jane*	36'		
2	Vito Dumas*	Arg	*Lehg II*	31' 2"	10' 9"	5' 8"
3	Marcel Bardiaux*	Fr	*Les Quatre Vents*	30' 8"	8' 10"	5' 9"
4	Bill Watson	GB	*Freedom*	34'		
5	Bill Nance	Aus	*Cardinal Vertue*	25' 3"	7' 2"	4' 6"
6	Edward Allcard*	GB	*Sea Wanderer*	36'	11'	5' 4"
7	Francis Chichester*	GB	*Gipsy Moth IV*	53' 1"	10' 6"	7' 9"

Rig	*Direc-tion*	*Date of Rounding*	*Great Capes*[1]	*Remarks*
Gaff yawl	W–E	Jan 16, 1911	1	First two-crew yacht round Cape Horn. First eastabout.
Gaff sloop	E–W	1934	1	First singlehanded rounding of Cape Horn. First westabout.
Bm. ketch	W–E	June 24, 1943	4	First solo eastabout. First to complete 'short' circumnavigation[2] east-about in high latitudes incl. Cape Horn. First round four Capes.
Bm. sloop	E–W	May 12, 1952	2	First solo to complete 'long' circumnavigation[2] westabout including rounding Cape Horn.
Gaff cutter	E–W W–E	Dec 25, 1962	1	Left yacht 1 mi. east of Cape, then rounded both ways in folding canoe; also swam off Cape Horn.
Bm. sloop	W–E	Jan 7, 1965	3	First solo to complete 'long' circumnavigation eastabout mostly in high latitudes after rounding Cape Horn.
Bm. ketch	E–W	Apr 12, 1966	1	First British single-hander to round Cape Horn westabout during circumnavigation.
Bm. yawl	W–E	Mar 20, 1967	3	First solo to complete 'long' circumnavigation eastabout mostly in high latitudes after only one stopover, via three Capes.

177

8	Alec Rose*	GB	*Lively Lady*	36′	9′ 3″	6′ 8″
	Tom Harrison	GB	*Sundowner*	25′		
9	Robin Knox-Johnston*	GB	*Suhaili*	32′ 5″	11′ 1″	5′ 6″
10	Bernard Moitessier*	IC/ Fr	*Joshua*	39′ 6″	12′	5′ 3″
11	Nigel Tetley*	GB	*Victress* (tri)	40′	22′	2′ 9″
12	Chay Blyth*	GB	*British Steel*	59′	12′ 10″	8′
13	Hiroshi Aoki	Jap	*Ahodori II*	20′ 9″	6′ 8″	4′ 3″
14	Bill King*	Eire/ GB	*Galway Blazer II*	42′	10′ 6″	6′ 1″

Bm. yawl	W–E	Apr 1, 1968	4	First solo to complete 'long' circumnavigation eastabout mostly in high latitudes after only one stopover, via four Capes.
Bm. sloop	E–W	May 1968		*Requires confirmation*
Bm. ketch	W–E	Jan 17, 1969	3	First to complete 'long' circumnavigation solo eastabout mostly in high latitudes, non-stop, via three Capes. Longest time, 313 days at sea.
Bm. ketch	W–E	Feb 5, 1969	5 + 4	First solo non-stop circumnavigation ('short'). First south of nine Capes non-stop, sailing nearly 38,000 miles: longest distance. First steel yacht.
Bm. ketch	W–E	Mar 18, 1969	5	First solo non-stop rounding of five Capes. First tri. First multihull to make 'long' solo circumnavigation. Sunk off Azores.
Bm. ketch	E–W	Dec 24, 1970	4	First solo to complete 'long' circumnavigation westabout mostly in Roaring Forties via four Capes. Largest monohull. Second steel yacht.
Bm. yawl	W–E	Jan 12, 1973	3	Smallest yacht to round Cape Horn under sail (see no. 4)
Two-masted junk-rigged sch.	W–E	Feb 5, 1973	5	First solo and lightest displacement ($4\frac{1}{2}$ tons) to round all five Capes and return to home port after circumnavigation

15	Kris Baranowski	Pol	*Polonez*	45′ 3″	12′ 5″	7′ 3″
16	Kenichi Horie*	Jap	*Mermaid III*	28′ 10″	9′ 3″	5′ 5″
17	Ryusuke Ushijima	Jap	*Gingitsune*	31′	9′ 10″	4′ 7″
18	Ambrogio Fogar	It	*Suprise*	38′ 8″	11′ 2″	6′ 2″
19	Alain Colas	Fr	*Manureva* (tri)	70′	35′	9′
20	Jorgen Meyer	Ger	*Butera*	52′ 6″	12′ 6″	7′ 9″

[1]Sailing eastabout, the five great Capes which must be rounded to complete a circumnavigation entirely in the Roaring Forties are: Good Hope (South Africa), Leeuwin (SW Australia), South East Cape (South Tasmania), South West Cape (South Stewart Island, NZ), and Cape Horn.

Bm. ketch	W–E	Feb 23, 1973	5	Record solo monohull passage: Hobart to Horn, 45 days (fastest with crew, 25 days—Apx. 6)
Bm. sloop	E–W	Jan 5, 1974	2	First solo to sail through a position antipodean to the home port during a 'long' circumnavigation via Horn (34°40′N, 135°30′E: start at Osaka)
Bm. ketch	W–E	Jan 15, 1974	2	Left Hakata, Japan Aug 27, 1973 for non-stop circumnavigation. Put into East London, SA Apr 29, 1974 for repairs after 245 days at sea.
Bm. sloop	E–W	Jan 27, 1974	2	After rounding Horn, capsized on Feb 2 and rammed by whale on Mar 7
Bm. ketch	W–E	Feb 4, 1974	3	Record solo passage: Sydney to Cape Horn 37 days (no. 15 above)
	E–W	1975		(*Awaiting further information of this non-stop circumnavigation attempt.*)

[2]The distinction between 'short' and 'long' circumnavigations was proposed by Sir Francis Chichester, in a letter to the author in which he suggested that a true circumnavigation should pass through two points antipodean to each other on the earth's surface.

Transatlantic Marine Records

SAIL

Record	Direc-tion	Date	Crew
First two-crew	W–E	1857	C R Webb and crew (USA)
First two-crew	E–W	1870	John Buckley (USA); Nicholas Primoraz (A)
First solo (after Slocum)	W–E	1876	Alfred Johnson (Dk/USA)
First solo	E–W	1923	Alain Gerbault* (Fr)
First double crossing (and smallest E–W by N route)	W–E	1880	F Norman (GB); G P Thomas (Can)
	E–W	1881	
First double crossing by sailing canoe	E–W	1904	John C Voss* (USA); E Harrison (Aus)
	W–E	1904	
First woman, etc		*see Apx. 9*	
First trimaran	W–E	1868	John Mikes (USA) and two crew (Prussia)
Earliest modern trimaran	E–W	1946	André Sadrin and two crew (Fr)
Earliest modern catamaran	E–W	1950–1	Raoul Christiaen, wife and two crew (Fr)
First solo trimaran	E–W	1964	Derek Kelsall (GB)
First solo catamaran	E–W	1964	David Lewis (NZ)

Vessel	LOA	Route	Days
Charter Oak	43′	New York–Liverpool	35
City of Ragusa	20′	Liverpool–Cork–Boston	8 + 84
Centennial	20′	Gloucester, Mass.–Shag Harbour, Maine–Abercastle–Liverpool	7 + 46 + 2
Firecrest	39′	Gibraltar–New York	101
Little Western	16′	Gloucester, Mass.–Cowes, IOW	46
Little Western	16′	London–Halifax, NS	79
Tilikum	38′	Cape Town–St Helena–Pernambuco	17 + 18
Tilikum	38′	Pernambuco–Ponta Delgada (Azores)–Margate (on Thames Estuary)	60 + 20
Nonpareil (inflatable)	25′	New York–Southampton	51
Ananda	42′ 10″	(Sète–Casablanca)–Cape Verde Is.–Fort de France	20
Copula	47′ 8″	(Bordeaux)–Santa Cruz–Martinique–(New York)	31
Folatre	35′	Plymouth, Devon–Newport, RI (2nd OSTAR)	35
Rehu Moana	40′	Plymouth–Newport (2nd OSTAR)	$38\frac{1}{2}$

First catamaran double crossing	E–W W–E	1956–7 1959	James Wharram (GB); Ruth Merseberger, Jutta Schultze-**Rhonof (Ger)**
Fastest solo monohull	W–E	1922	J V T McDonald (GB)
Fastest solo monohull	E–W	1970	Sir Francis Chichester*, KBE (GB)
Fastest solo multihull	E–W	1972	Alain Colas (Fr)
Fastest crewed multihull	E–W	1968	Eric Tabarly and two crew (Fr)
Fastest crewed monohull	W–E	1905	Captain and crew (USA)
Fastest small clipper	E–W	1824	Captain and crew (USA)
Fastest small barque	E–W	1830	Captain and crew (USA)
Fastest large clipper	E–W	1860	Captain and crew (USA)
Fastest large clipper	W–E	1854	Captain and crew (USA)
Claimed fastest-ever crossing	W–E	1916	Captain and crew (Nor)
Largest solo yacht	E–W	1972	Jean-Yves Terlain (Fr)
Smallest solo yacht	W–E	1966	William Verity (USA)
Smallest solo yacht	E–W	1968	Hugo Vihlen (USA)
Most solo crossings		1937–73	Jean Gau (Fr/USA)

Tangaroa	23' 6"	Las Palmas–Trinidad	41
Rongo	40'	New York–Liverpool	50
Inverarity	38'	Halifax, NS–Ireland	16
Gipsy Moth V	57'	Portuguese Guinea–Nicaragua (171·9 m.p.d.)	$22\frac{1}{6}$
Pen Duick IV (tri)	70'	Plymouth, Devon–Newport, RI (first in 4th OSTAR) (145 m.p.d.)	$20\frac{1}{2}$
Pen Duick IV (tri)	70'	Tenerife–Martinique (253·8 m.p.d.)	$10\frac{1}{2}$
Atlantic (three-mast sch.)	185'	Sandy Hook, NY–Lizard (fastest noon-noon 341 mi.)	$12\frac{1}{6}$
Emerald	110'	Liverpool–Boston (192·9 m.p.d.)	17
Josephine	86'	Belfast–New York (193·8 m.p.d.)	16
Andrew Jackson	1679 tons	Liverpool–New York (207·1 m.p.d.)	15
Red Jacket	2434 tons	Sandy Hook–Bell Buoy, Liverpool (277·7 m.p.d.)	12
Lancing	405'	Sandy Hook–Cape Wrath, Scotland (17·3 knots)	$6\frac{3}{4}$
Vendredi 13	128'	Plymouth–Newport (second in 4th OSTAR)	$21\frac{1}{5}$
Nonoalca	12'	Fort Lauderdale, Fl.–Tralee, Eire	68
April Fool	6'	Casablanca–Miami	84
Atom (mostly)	30'	12 crossings from/to various ports in both directions	

185

Fastest solo yacht noon-noon	N–S	1973	Alain Colas (Fr)
Fastest crewed yacht (three days)	E–W	1968	Eric Tabarly and two crew (Fr)
Youngest solo	E–W	1967	Robin Lee Graham* (USA): age $18\frac{1}{2}$
Oldest solo	W–E	1973	Jean Gau (Fr/USA): age nearly 72
Fastest solo yacht noon-noon	N–S	1975	Nick Keig (GB)

ROWING AND POWER

First recorded solo canoe	W–E	1682	'Finn-man' (probably Eskimo)
First rowing	E–W	1799	Six British deserters from garrison
First two-crew rowing	W–E	1896	George Harbo; Frank Samuelson (Nor/USA)
First British two-crew rowing	W–E	1966	John Ridgeway*; Chay Blyth (GB)

Manureva (tri) (ex *Pen Duick IV*)	70′	In South Atlantic: 326 mi. in 24 hr	
Pen Duick IV (tri)	70′	Sailed 930 mi. in 72 hr: av. 310 m.p.d.	
Dove	24′	Cape Town–Ascension– Paramaribo (–Barbados)	38
Atom	30′	New York towards France. Wrecked on N African coast.	
Three Legs of Mann (tri)	35′	Azores and Back Singlehanded Race (AZAB): 328 mi.	
kayak	20′ approx	Arrived Orkneys; others reported	
ship's boat	20′ approx	St Helena–Ascension– Belmonte, Brazil (83 m.p.d.)	8 + 20
Richard K Fox	18′ 4″	New York–Scilly Isles– Le Havre (56 m.p.d.)	55 + 4
English Rose III	20′	Cape Cod–Inishmore, Eire (31 m.p.d.)	91

First solo rowing	E–W	1969	John Fairfax* (GB)
First solo rowing	W–E	1969	Tom McClean* (Eire)
Longest solo row (and fastest)	E–W	1970	Sidney Genders (GB)
Earliest modern canoe (small sail)	E–W	1928	Franz Romer (Ger)
Smallest canoe (small sail)	E–W	1956	Hannes Lindemann* (Ger)
First motor boat	W–E	1902	William Newman and son Edward (16) (USA)
First solo motor boat	W–E	1936	Marin-Marie* (Fr)
First solo motor boat	E–W	1957	Walter Westborg (Dk)
Amphibious Jeep	W–E	1950	Ben Carlin* and wife Elinore (Aus)
Rubber dinghy (no food or water)	E–W	1952	Dr Alain Bombard* (Fr)
First solo raft	E–W	1957–9	René Lescomb (Fr)

A	Austria	Dk	Denmark
Aus	Australia	NZ	New Zealand
Can	Canada	NS	Nova Scotia

Britannia	22′	Las Palmas–Fort Lauderdale, Fla. (20 m.p.d.)	181
Super Silver	20′	St Johns, Newfoundland–Blacksod Bay, Eire (24 m.p.d.)	$70\frac{3}{4}$
Khaggavisana	19′ 9″	Sennen Cove, Cornwall–Canaries–Antigua–Miami (37 m.p.d.)	140
Deutscheir Sport	21′ 6″	Lisbon–Cape St Vincent–Canaries–St Thomas (47 m.p.d.)	6 + 11 + 58
Liberia III (collapsible)	17′	Las Palmas–St Martin (40 m.p.d.)	71
Abiel Abbott Low	42′	New York–Falmouth	36
Arielle	43′	New York–Le Havre	$18\frac{3}{4}$
Dana Rescuer	23′	(Esbjerg–Margate–Cherbourg–Brest–Lisbon–Canaries)–Cape Verde–Panama	33
Half-Safe	18′ 3″	Halifax, NS–Azores–Madeira–Cape Juby, W Africa	$31 + 23\frac{1}{2} + 1\frac{1}{2}$
L'Hérétique	15′	Casablanca–Las Palmas–Barbados	$11 + 64\frac{1}{2}$
Pot-au-Noir I and *II*		(Bordeaux–Gijon)–Canaries–Barbados	50

Daily averages are for the most part approximate, based on direct route mileages. All figures in nautical miles.

189

Transpacific Yacht Records

Record	Date	Crew
First non-stop solo sail (E–W)	1882–3	Bernard Gilboy* (USA)
First solo sail (W–E) and smallest	1932–3	Fred Rebell* (born Latvia)
Smallest sail (E–W) and smallest ever	1970	John Riding (GB)
Smallest non-stop solo, North Pacific	1967	Ikuo Kashima (Jap)
First solo sail (W–E) from Japan	1932	Edward Miles (USA)
First solo woman		Sharon Sites (see Apx. 9)
First solo raft (E–W)	1954	William Willis* (USA)
First raft double crossing	1956–7 1958	Eric de Bisschop* (Fr) and four crew on both voyages (de Bisschop lost on second voyage)
First rowing and longest two-crew row	1971–2	John Fairfax*; Sylvia Cook (GB)
First two-crew (E–W)	1901	John Voss* (Ger/USA); Norman Luxton (Can) to Fiji. Louis Begent (Tas) lost overboard
First two-crew (W–E)	1910–11	George Blythe (GB); Peter Arapakis (Gk/Aus).
Earliest modern multihull	1937–8	Eric de Bisschop; Joseph Tatibouet (Fr)

Craft	LOA	Route	Days
Pacific	18′	San Francisco–off Queensland, Aus.	162
Elaine	18′	Sydney, Aus.–San Pedro (incl. stops)	372
Sjö Äg	12′	San Diego–New Zealand (lost in Tasman Sea)	
Koraassa II	16′ 5″	Los Angeles–Yokohama	101
Sturdy II	36′ 9″	Yokohama–Honolulu–San Francisco	58 + 18
Sea Sharp		*see Apx. 9*	
Seven Little Sisters	33′	Callao, Peru–Pago Pago, Samoa	115
Tahiti-Nui I *Tahiti-Nui II*		Tahiti–Juan Fernandex Chile–Rakahanga, Cook Is.	203
Britannia II	35′	San Francisco–Hayman Is., Aus	362
Tilikum	38′	Victoria, BC–Sydney, Aus (incl. stops). Fastest day's run 177 miles. (Apx. 3)	144
Pandora	36′ 9″	Bunbury, W Australia–Melbourne–Sydney–Auckland–Pitcairn–Easter Is.–Cape Horn	258
Kaimiloa (cat)	38′	Hawaii–Torres Strait–Cape of Good Hope–Cannes (incl. stops).	264

Appendix 6

Fastest trimaran	1969	Eric Tabarly* and two crew (Fr)
Fastest monohull	1973–4	Chay Blyth* and nine crew (GB)
Fastest singlehanded monohull	1969	Eric Tabarly* (Fr)

Pen Duick IV	70′	Los Angeles–Honolulu (av. 260·5 m.p.d.). Fastest clipper *Swordfish*, 1036 tons, San Francisco–Honolulu in 8 days, 2 hr (av. 259·2 m.p.d.); 1853.	$8\frac{1}{2}$
Great Britain II	72′	Sydney–Cape Horn. Fastest clipper *Lightning*, 2084 tons, Melbourne–Horn in 19 days, 1 hr; 1854.	25
Pen Duick V	35′	Winner first Singlehanded Transpacific Race San Francisco–Misaki, Tokyo Bay. Record time: 39 days, 15 hr, 44 min.	$39\frac{2}{3}$

E.S.H.—O

Trans-Indian Ocean

Record	Date	Crew
Earliest yacht record crossing	1853	L B Hodge and crew (USA)
First two-crew (W–E)	1889–90	Turgen Englehardt (Scan) Neilson (Scan)
First two-crew (E–W)	1902	John Voss* (Ger/USA) 'Mac' MacMillen (NZ)
First solo (E–W)	1897	Joshua Slocum* (NS/USA)
First solo (W–E)	1930–1	Edward Miles (USA)
Earliest modern multihull	1937–8	Eric de Bisschop (Fr) Joseph Tatibouet (Fr)
Earliest solo multihull	1966–7	Tom Corkhill (Aus)
First solo rowing	1971	Anders Svedlund (Swed)

Craft	*LOA*	*Route*	*Days*
Pride of the Sea (sch.)	97'	Cape of Good Hope–Melbourne (av. 210 m.p.d.). Fastest clipper *Red Jacket*, 2305 tons, 19 days, 15 hr; 1854 (av. 284 m.p.d.).	29
Stormking (steel)	40'	London–Cape Town–Adelaide	124 + 111
Tilikum	38'	Thursday Is.–Rodriguez Is.–Durban, SA (incl. stops—see Apx. 3)	67 + 30
Spray	36' 9"	Thursday Is.–Rodriguez Is.–Mauritius–Durban, SA	23 + 16 + 3 + 22
Sturdy II	36' 9"	Port Tewfik, Egypt–India–Ceylon–Singapore (incl. many stops)	300 (approx.)
Kaimiloa (cat)	38'	Hawaii–Torres Strait–Cape of Good Hope–Cannes (incl. other stops)	264
Clipper I (tri)	25'	Thursday Is.–Darwin–(Kupang–Sumbawa–) Singapore–Mauritius (fastest day's run 203 mi.)–Durban, SA	12 + 62 + 21
		Australia–Madagascar (*further information required*)	

Singlehanded Transocean Races

TRANSATLANTIC RACES

Race	Order of finishing	Flag	Yacht (LOA)	Start
1	J W Lawlor	USA	Sea Serpent (15')	
	W A Andrews	USA	Mermaid (15')	Boston, Mass.
2	W A Andrews	USA	Sapolio (14' 6")	
	J W Lawlor	USA	Christopher Columbus (16')	Atlantic City, NJ
3	Howard Blackburn*	USA	Great Republic (25')	Gloucester, Mass.
4	Peter Tangvald*	USA	Windflower (45')	
	Edward Allcard*	GB	Sea Wanderer (36')	Las Palmas, Canary Is.
5	Francis Chichester*	GB	Gipsy Moth III (39' 7")	
	Blondie Hasler	GB	Jester (25' 9")	Plymouth, Devon
	David Lewis*	GB	Cardinal Vertue (25' 3")	
6	Eric Tabarly*	Fr	Pen Duick II (44')	
	Francis Chichester	GB	Gipsy Moth III (39' 7")	Plymouth, Devon
	Val Howells	GB	Akka (35')	

Date	Finish	Date	Days	Remarks
June 21, 1891	Coverack, Devon	Aug 5, 1891	45	Winner of first STR
June 21, 1891	At sea	Aug 22, 1891	61	Picked up after capsizing by *SS Ebruz* within 600 mi. of finish
July 20, 1892	Palos, Spain	Sept 27, 1892	69	Stopped three days at Terceira, Azores. Actual sailing time 66 days.
July 2, 1892				Lost at sea
June 9, 1901	Cape Espichel, Portugal	July 17, 1901	38	Issued STR challenge through press, via East Gloucester Yacht Club, on Jan 1, 1901. No takers, so raced against clock.
Nov 20, 1957	English Harbour, Antigua	Dec 21, 1957	31	Raced for $1 stake—loser to pay. Allcard allowed to use auxiliary engine as his was smaller vessel.
		Dec 23, 1957	33	
June 11, 1960	New York	July 21, 1960	40	First Observer Singlehanded Transatlantic Race. 5 started, 5 completed race. Last to finish: Jean Lacombe's 21' *Cape Horn* taking 74 days.
		July 30, 1960	48	
		Aug 6, 1960	56	
May 23, 1964	Newport, RI	June 19, 1964	27	Second OSTAR. 15 started, 14 completed race. Last to finish: Axel Pederson's 28' *Marco Polo* taking 63 days.
		June 22, 1964	29	
		June 25, 1964	32	

7	Geoffrey Williams*	GB	*Sir Thomas Lipton* (57′)	
	Bruce Dalling	GB	*Voortrekker* (50′)	Plymouth, Devon
	Tom Follett*	USA	*Cheers* (proa) (40′)	
8	Alain Colas	Fr	*Pen Duick IV* (tri) (70′)	
	Jean-Yves Terlain	Fr	*Vendredi 13* (128′)	Plymouth, Devon
	Jean Marie Vidal	Fr	*Cap 33* (tri) (52′ 9″)	

TRANSPACIFIC RACES

Eric Tabarly*	Fr	*Pen Duick V* (35′)	
Jean-Y Terlain	Fr	*Blue Arpege* (30′)	San Francisco
Claus Hehner	Ger	*Mex* (35′)	

ROUND-THE-WORLD RACE

Robin Knox-Johnston	GB	*Suhaili* (32′ 5″)	Falmouth, Cornwall.

June 1, 1968	Newport, RI	June 27, 1968	25	Third OSTAR (only 27 hr, 40 min separated first three home). 35 started, 19 completed race. Last to finish: Michael Richey's 25′ *Jester* (ex-Hasler's) in 57 days.
		June 27, 1968	26	
		June 28, 1968	26	
June 17, 1972	Newport, RI	July 7, 1972	20	Fourth OSTAR: 54 started, 40 completed race within time limit of 60 days, 3 outside time limit. Official last: Anne Michailof's 30′ 8″ *P.S.* taking 59 days. Actual last: Peter Crowther's 38′ gaff cutter *Golden Vanity*.
		July 8, 1972	21	
		July 11, 1972	24	
Mar 15, 1969	Misaki, Tokyo Bay	Apr 24, 1969	40	First Singlehanded Trans-pacific Race. 5 started, 4 completed course. Winner holds record for fastest solo Pacific crossing (39 days, 15 hr, 44 min).
		May 5, 1969	52	
		May 7, 1969	54	
June 14, 1968	Falmouth, Cornwall	Apr 22, 1969	313	First Singlehanded Round-the-world Race. Seven monohulls and two trimarans started; only *Suhaili* finished.

Transocean Yachtswomen

	Name	Nation-ality	Yacht	LOA	Beam	Draft
Two crew	Thomas Crapo Joanna (wife)	USA Scot	New Bedford	19' 7"	6' 2"	1' 1"
Two crew	Roger Strout Edith (wife)	USA	Igdrasil	36' 9"	14' 2"	4' 2"
	Gladys Gradely			18' approx		
1	Ann Davison*	GB	Felicity Ann	23'	7' 6"	4' 6"
2	Sharon Sites	USA	Sea Sharp	25'	9'	3' 6"
3	Sharon Sites Adams*	USA	Sea Sharp II	30' 10"	9' 9"	3' 9"

Rig	Direc-tion	Year	Days	Remarks
Bm. sch.	W–E	1877	51	First couple alone transocean. First woman across Atlantic in two-crew small boat. First bermudan rig transatlantic.
Gaff yawl	E W	1934–7		First couple to make circumnavigation alone. First woman circumnavigator in two-crew small boat. Distance 37,000 mi. First couple to receive CCA Blue Water Medal.
Lug	W–E	About 1903	60	First transatlantic crossing by solo woman, but requires more confirmation. Nova Scotia to Hope Cove, Devon. Time approximate.
Bm. sloop	E–W	1952–3	454	First confirmed solo Atlantic crossing. From Plymouth, via Douarnenez, Vigo, Gibraltar, Casablanca, Las Palmas, Dominica, Bahamas, Miami to New York.
Bm. sloop	E–W	1965	39	First solo Pacific crossing by a woman. From Marina del Rey, near Santa Monica, Calif. to Honolulu in 39 days, $4\frac{1}{2}$ hr: 2480 mi.
Bm. ketch	W–E	1969	75	First W–E Pacific crossing by solo woman. Longest voyage and longest time at sea by solo woman. Yokohama to San Diego: 5900 mi. First Pacific double crossing by solo woman.

4	Ingeborg von Heister	Ger	*Ultima Ratio* (tri)	35'	20'	2' 6"
5	Ingeborg von Heister	Ger	*Ultima Ratio* (tri)	35'	20'	2' 6"
6	Nicolette Milnes Walker*	GB	*Aziz*	30'	8'	4' 4"
7	Marie-Claude Fauroux	Fr	*Aloa VII*	34' 9"	11'	5' 10"
8	Teresa Remiszewska	Pol	*Komodor*	42'	10' 3"	6' 6"
9	Anne Michailof	Fr	*P.S.*	30' 8"	10' 6"	5' 7"
10	Clare Francis*	GB	*Gulliver G*	32'	9' 6"	5' 6"
11	Annette Wilde	NZ	*Valya*	33'	10' 8"	5' 6"

Bm. ketch	E–W	1969	33	Second E–W Atlantic crossing by solo woman: Las Palmas–Barbados 33 days. Sailed solo from Britain to Mediterranean in 1966.
Bm. ketch	W–E	1970	46	First W–E confirmed Atlantic crossing by solo woman—from Bermuda, via Azores to Gibraltar. First double crossing of Atlantic by solo woman.
Bm. sloop	E–W	1971	44	Third E–W Atlantic crossing by solo woman; first non-stop from Britain to America via southern route: 3400 mi.
Bm. sloop	E–W	1972	33	1972 OSTAR. Finished fourteenth. Plymouth to Newport: fourth E–W Atlantic crossing by solo woman; first French solo woman trans-ocean.
Bm. yawl	E–W	1972	57	1972 OSTAR. Finished thirty-eighth. Plymouth to Newport: fifth E–W Atlantic crossing by solo woman; first Polish solo woman transocean.
Bm. sloop	E–W	1972	59	1972 OSTAR. Finished fortieth. Plymouth to Newport: sixth E–W Atlantic crossing by solo woman.
Bm. sloop	E–W	1973	37	Falmouth to Newport via southern route. Smallest woman (5′ 2″, only 105 lb). Returned via West Indies with crew.
Bm. sloop	E–W W–E	1974	$14\frac{1}{2}$ 18	First double crossing of Tasman Sea by solo woman. New Plymouth–Brisbane–Christchurch. Ferrocement yacht (9 tons) home built by Annette and friend.

Singlehanded Blue Water Medallists

The Blue Water Medal

'Feeling that there were many noteworthy voyages made in small boats, and frequent examples of meritorious seamanship displayed by amateur sailors of all nationalities that went unrecognized, it seemed to the members of The Cruising Club of America that this organization was the fitting one properly to record and reward such adventure upon the sea.

Therefore, at the annual meeting on February 27, 1923 the following resolution was passed, founding a medal that, it was hoped, might prove an incentive for carrying on the spirit of adventure and upholding the best traditions of seafaring that are our heritage from the past.

> Moved and seconded that the Club found, out of funds to be sought for the purpose, a medal to be known as "The Blue Water Medal of The Cruising Club of America", to be awarded annually, in the discretion of the Board of Governors, for the year's most meritorious example of seamanship, the recipient to be selected from among the amateurs of all the nations.

In pursuance of this resolution a suitable medal, five inches in diameter, was made, designed by the late Arthur Sturgis Hildebrand, a member of the club and one of the crew of the yacht *Leiv Eiriksson*, lost in the Arctic with all hands in September 1924.'

Singlehanded Blue Water Medal Awards

1923   *Firecrest*   Alain J Gerbault   France
Left Gibraltar June 7, 1923 and arrived Fort Totten, Long Island exactly 100 days later. Non-stop. Dixon Kemp-designed British cutter, 34 ft overall. Singlehanded.

1925   *Islander*   Harry Pidgeon   USA
First circumnavigation—from Los Angeles to Los Angeles via Cape and Panama Canal, November 18,

1921 to October 31, 1925. Home-built 34 ft overall yawl of Sea Bird type. Singlehanded.

1934   *May L*   W B Reese   England
A singlehanded passage in a small double ended ketch from England in the fall of 1933 to Nassau in January 1934.

1936   *Arielle*   Marin-Marie   France
A singlehanded transatlantic passage in a 42 ft 7 in overall motor boat (July 23 to August 10, 1936) with two self-steering devices. Marie had sailed the cutter *Winnibelle II* (without power) from Brest to New York in 1933.

1952   *Stornoway*   Alfred Peterson   USA
A circumnavigation from and to New York via the two major canals in a 33 ft double ended cutter. Singlehanded, June 1948 to August 18, 1952.

1958   *Les Quatre Vents*   Marcel Bardiaux   France
Singlehanded circumnavigation westabout around Cape Horn and the Cape of Good Hope, in home-built sloop 30 ft 9 in overall. From Ouistreham, France May 24, 1950 to Arcachon, France July 25, 1958.

1959   *Trekka*   John Guzzwell   Canada
Singlehanded circumnavigation in home-built yawl 20 ft 10 in overall via the Cape of Good Hope and the Panama Canal. From Victoria, British Columbia to Victoria; September 10, 1955 to September 10, 1959.

Without date   *Legh I*, *Legh II*, *Sirio*   Vito Dumas   Argentine
Global circumnavigation in *Legh II*, 1942–3. Other phenomenal singlehanded voyages in *Legh I*, 1931–2; *Legh II*, 1945–7; *Sirio*, 1955.

1960   *Gypsy Moth III*   Francis Chichester   England
Winner of the first Singlehanded Race across the Atlantic in 1960, from east to west across the Atlantic.

1964   *Pen Duick III*   Eric Tabarly   France
Winner of the second Singlehanded Race across the Atlantic from Plymouth, England to Newport, Rhode Island in twenty-seven days, one hour, fifty-six minutes.

1967   *Gipsy Moth IV*   Sir Francis Chichester   England
Singlehanded passage around the world, via the Cape of Good Hope and Cape Horn. Stopping only at Sydney, Australia, the distance was 29,630 miles for the whole voyage.

1968   *Lively Lady*   Sir Alec Rose   England
Singlehanded circumnavigation of the world with stops only at Melbourne, Australia and Bluff, New Zealand. He departed Portsmouth, England on July 16, 1967 and returned to that port on July 4, 1968.

1970   *Elsie*   Frank Casper   USA
Extended singlehanded cruising including one circumnavigation and numerous transatlantic passages.

The above details were very kindly supplied by the Secretary of The Cruising Club of America, who gave me permission to publish them. However, several facts and figures quoted in this list are inaccurate and so the details should not be taken as necessarily correct. E.g. *Firecrest* was 39 ft overall; Vito Dumas called his yachts *Lehg*—not *Legh*. However, I thought it best to publish this list exactly as supplied, because although I believe my facts are more accurate I would never be entirely dogmatic about *any* details connected with small boats and their voyages: there is always far too much conflicting evidence for anyone to be absolutely certain.

For those who are interested in the history of small boat voyaging, the only organization in the world which specializes in the subject is:

The Slocum Society
Ken Baker, Secretary
P.O. Box 857
Hilo, Hawaii, 96720, USA